New Day

C000134911

Edited by **Gordon Giles**

January–April 2024

 **Ministries**

15 The Chambers, Vineyard,
Abingdon OX14 3FE
brf.org.uk

Bible Reading Fellowship is a charity (233280)
and company limited by guarantee (301324),
registered in England and Wales

ISBN 978 1 80039 258 8
All rights reserved

This edition © Bible Reading Fellowship 2023
Cover photo by Flickr/pexels.com

Distributed in Australia by:
MediaCom Education Inc, PO Box 610, Unley, SA 5061
Tel: 1 800 811 311 | admin@mediacom.org.au

Distributed in New Zealand by:
Scripture Union Wholesale, PO Box 760, Wellington 6140
Tel: 04 385 0421 | suwholesale@clear.net.nz

Acknowledgements
Scripture quotations marked NRSV are taken from the New Revised Standard
Version Updated Edition. Copyright © 2021 National Council of Churches of Christ
in the United States of America. Used by permission. All rights reserved worldwide.

Scripture quotations marked NIV are taken from The Holy Bible, New International
Version, Anglicised edition, copyright © 1979, 1984, 2011 by Biblica. Used by
permission of Hodder & Stoughton Publishers, an Hachette UK company. All rights
reserved. 'NIV' is a registered trademark of Biblica. UK trademark number 1448790.

A catalogue record for this book is available from the British Library

Printed by Gutenberg Press, Tarxien, Malta

Suggestions for using *New Daylight*

Find a regular time and place, if possible, where you can read and pray undisturbed. Before you begin, take time to be still and perhaps use the prayer of BRF Ministries on page 6. Then read the Bible passage slowly (try reading it aloud if you find it over-familiar), followed by the comment. You can also use *New Daylight* for group study and discussion, if you prefer.

The prayer or point for reflection can be a starting point for your own meditation and prayer. Many people like to keep a journal to record their thoughts about a Bible passage and items for prayer. In *New Daylight* we also note the Sundays and some special festivals from the church calendar, to keep in step with the Christian year.

New Daylight and the Bible

New Daylight contributors use a range of Bible versions, and you will find a list of the versions used opposite. You are welcome to use your own preferred version alongside the passage printed in the notes. This can be particularly helpful if the Bible text has been abridged.

New Daylight affirms that the whole of the Bible is God's revelation to us, and we should read, reflect on and learn from every part of both Old and New Testaments. Usually the printed comment presents a straightforward 'thought for the day', but sometimes it may also raise questions rather than simply providing answers, as we wrestle with some of the more difficult passages of scripture.

New Daylight is also available in a compact size edition. Visit your local Christian bookshop or BRF's online shop **brfonline.org.uk**. To obtain an audio version for the blind or partially sighted, contact Torch Trust for the Blind, Torch House, Torch Way, Northampton Road, Market Harborough LE16 9HL; +44 (0)1858 438260; **info@torchtrust.org**.

Comment on *New Daylight*

To send feedback, please email **enquiries@brf.org.uk**, phone **+44 (0)1865 319700** or write to the address shown opposite.

Writers in this issue

Amy Boucher Pye is a writer, speaker and spiritual director. She's the author of seven books, including the new *Holding Onto Hope* (BRF, 2023). Find her at **amyboucherpye.com**.

Terry Hinks is a United Reformed Church minister, serving two churches in Buckinghamshire. His love of the Bible, stillness and prayer has led him to writing many prayers and meditations, including *Praying the Way* (BRF, 2018).

Liz Hoare teaches on prayer and spirituality at Wycliffe Hall, Oxford. The author of *Twelve Great Spiritual Writers* (SPCK, 2020), she has worked in parish ministry and has a special interest in spiritual direction.

Tony Horsfall is an author, retreat leader and mentor based in Bournemouth. Among his many books published with BRF are *Mentoring Conversations*, *Working from a Place of Rest, Rhythms of Grace* and *Grief Notes*.

Emma Pennington is canon missioner of Canterbury Cathedral. Formerly a parish priest, area dean and spirituality adviser in the diocese of Oxford, she is the author of *At the Foot of the Cross with Julian of Norwich* (BRF, 2020).

Roland Riem is vice dean of Winchester Cathedral. Roland is currently also studying and teaching on Matthew's gospel, with a focus on the parables and Jewish-Christian relations.

David Runcorn is an Anglican priest, an author, a spiritual director and a retreat leader. His ministry has included local churches, Lee Abbey chaplain and a director of ordinands. You can meet him at **davidruncorn.com**.

Elizabeth Rundle has written many study and devotional books, including *20 Questions Jesus Asked* for BRF, has written and presented scripts for local and national radio and television, and led 16 pilgrimages to the Holy Land.

Sheila Walker is a former associate priest with three rural churches. She has worked as a teacher, editor, careers adviser, information officer, librarian and writer; also as wife, widow, single parent and stepmother, and grandmother.

Sally Welch is diocesan canon of Christ Church Cathedral, Oxford and co-director of the Centre for Christian Pilgrimage. She is the former editor of *New Daylight*.

Gordon Giles writes...

Happy New Year! I hope and pray that Christmas was a blessed time for you. It is easy – tempting even – to behave as though Christmastide ends on Boxing Day, but 26 December is in fact the feast of Stephen, and we begin this year with St Stephen, whose witness to Christ occupies the early chapters of Acts.

Exactly a week after Christmas comes New Year's Day, which few think of as having religious or spiritual significance. Not so! 1 January is the feast of the circumcision of Christ or 'the naming of Jesus', the two phenomena being simultaneous in Jewish tradition. The first is an act with religious and cultural heritage and significance. The second is more spiritual, but has deep impact on the life of the one who is named; what we are called affects how others think of us, and what others think of us affects how we perceive ourselves.

The act of circumcision had practical, precautionary benefit and cultural significance: it is the sign of covenant, dating back to Abraham. Doing it to Jesus *made him a Jew*, cementing that aspect of his identity. His virgin birth cemented his identity as Son of God. It is vital to our understanding of Jesus that he has Jewish heritage, not as a visitor to it, but as a real member born into that faith community. His identity is also glued to his name: it sets him apart, for he is not named after his earthly father, Joseph, but after his heavenly Father, the Lord God Almighty.

The meaning of the name 'Jesus', *Yeshua* (or Joshua), refers to salvation, to crying for help and having one's cries for help heard by almighty God. It is a universal name, sounding similar in almost every known language, whether spelt with a 'J', a 'G' or an 'I' at the beginning. In Aragonese (the region of Spain from which Henry VIII's first wife Katherine hailed), it is spelt *Chesús*. Indeed in some Latin American cultures, Jesus as a man's Christian name is acceptable and quite common, while in many other countries to name a child 'Jesus' would be peculiar.

Our Lord Jesus Christ crosses all these cultures and bears his name of salvation to all the corners of the earth, the sins of which he takes away. In a sense then, there can be no better 'Christian' name than that of Jesus!

GORDON GILES

The prayer of BRF Ministries

Faithful God,
thank you for growing BRF
from small beginnings
into a worldwide family of ministries.
We rejoice as young and old
discover you through your word
and grow daily in faith and love.
Keep us humble in your service,
ambitious for your glory
and open to new opportunities.
For your name's sake,
Amen.

'It is such a joy to be part of this amazing project'

As part of our Living Faith ministry, we're raising funds to give away copies of Bible reading notes and other resources to those who aren't able to access them any other way, working with food banks and chaplaincy services, in prisons, hospitals and care homes.

'This very generous gift will be hugely appreciated, and truly bless each recipient… Bless you for your kindness.'

'We would like to send our enormous thanks to all involved. Your generosity will have a significant impact and will help us to continue to provide support to local people in crisis, and for this we cannot thank you enough.'

If you've enjoyed and benefited from our resources, would you consider paying it forward to enable others to do so too?

Make a gift at **brf.org.uk/donate**

Stephen: Acts 6—7

 My wise New Testament tutor at theological college told us: 'The Bible doesn't tell us all we want to know, but it tells us all we *need* to know.' This is particularly pertinent to the story of Stephen. Who was this man who leaps from the page by strength of witness and tragic martyrdom hardly ever to be mentioned again? His appearance on the stage of the embryonic church is tantalisingly brief, yet his impact on the spread of the gospel is immeasurable.

What we call Boxing Day is also the feast of St Stephen. Maybe you have recently sung about king Wenceslas who 'looked out, on the feast of Stephen'. For many, this season has been a busy time and Stephen, this educated, Greek-speaking, courageous and Spirit-filled man, hardly gets a second thought before we hurtle into a new year. From their anointing of the Holy Spirit at Pentecost, Jesus' closest followers became known as apostles, meaning people sent out with a message. Today they would be called evangelists.

After the crucifixion of their master, and the death of Judas, Luke tells us the number of believers in Jerusalem numbered 120 people. From their number Matthias was chosen to take the place of Judas. But it is clear others had been with Jesus and witnessed his death and resurrection (see Acts 2:21–23). Had Stephen been one of those witnesses?

Luke, the author of Acts, does not gloss over the difficulties faced in those early days of the infant church. Beatings, imprisonment, deceit and jealousy dogged the groups endeavouring to live by the teaching of Jesus Christ. Charismatic Stephen stood out from the crowd for his faith, education, grace and power. He was the man for the moment – practical, spiritual and committed. Stephen's appearance in Acts is brief; nevertheless he played a critical role in the spread of the gospel. It is a role which is too often overshadowed and neglected. Stephen's influence was pivotal and worth considering anew.

I pray that as we tread into a new year, some of us apprehensively, some with deep anxiety and some looking forward to coming joys, we may discover a real person to inspire our own faith journey.

ELIZABETH RUNDLE

Growing pains

Every day in the temple and at home they did not cease to teach and proclaim Jesus as the Messiah. Now during those days, when the disciples were increasing in number, the Hellenists complained against the Hebrews because their widows were being neglected in the daily distribution of food. And the twelve called together the whole community… and said… 'Brothers and sisters, select from among yourselves seven men of good standing, full of the Spirit and of wisdom, whom we may appoint to this task.'

The book of Acts vividly combines the highs and lows of those early days and months following Jesus' crucifixion, resurrection and ascension. Two of Jesus' closest disciples, Peter and John, had been arrested, imprisoned, interrogated and flogged. It is truly disturbing that, as we begin 2024, in some 50 countries the same penalties are still meted out to Christians.

But what a miraculous response of Spirit-emboldened courage, then and now. Two words call out to me: 'temple' and 'home'. For these apostles their faith was their whole life. Wherever they were and whoever they were with, nothing would stop their witness to family, friends or strangers about Jesus the Messiah.

Sadly, no church growth comes without the growing pains of distractions, discontent and disappointment. Few of us can honestly say we adapt to change easily and without complaint. Perhaps it is a symptom of age, insecurity or stubbornness. Never had the people in Jerusalem heard such a radical message. The teaching, death and resurrection of Jesus of Nazareth would not only change lives but change history itself.

One short phrase, 'the daily distribution of food', reminds us of contemporary issues of need. The founder of The Salvation Army, William Booth, once said, 'You cannot warm the hearts of people with God's love if they have an empty stomach.' The living gospel was, is and always will be life-changing, holistic and inclusive.

What problems and resistance do today's congregations face? What do we need to change as we seek outreach and growth? Thank you, Lord, that your Holy Spirit still motivates believers into caring for those in need. Amen.

ELIZABETH RUNDLE

First of many

What they said pleased the whole community, and they chose Stephen, a man full of faith and the Holy Spirit, together with Philip, Prochorus, Nicanor, Timon, Parmenas, and Nicolaus, a proselyte of Antioch. They had these men stand before the apostles, who prayed and laid their hands on them. The word of God continued to spread; the number of the disciples increased greatly in Jerusalem, and a great many of the priests became obedient to the faith.

This was a crucial time for the early believers. The number of converts was growing at such a pace that the twelve apostles realised there was no way that on their own they could fulfill the spiritual and physical needs of them all. To build up the body of Christ, they needed to embrace the gifts God had given to others.

It is a grace to delegate. Maybe you can think of times when delegation would have helped a situation and enabled different people to share their own gifts. Although we are thinking of Stephen, I feel the other men's names are necessary to mention. Look again. They were not men from Galilee or Jerusalem, but Greek-speaking Jews brought up in other countries; one of them, Nicolaus, was a convert to Judaism. These seven men, chosen by the whole community, would be instrumental to the practical work of the gospel.

The apostles laid hands on them, the ancient Jewish practice to commission a person. For example, Moses laid his hands on Joshua, who is described in words similar to that used of Stephen: 'full of the spirit of wisdom' (Deuteronomy 34:9).

It is heartwarming to know that in each century, in every country and in every language, prayer and the laying on of hands have been signs of ordination. This young man, Stephen, was set apart and acknowledged as one of the first deacons, ordained to serve the new church families. The following verses tell us that 'the number of the disciples increased greatly' (v. 7), but also that, sadly, so did the opposition from the synagogue of the Freedmen.

Forgive me, Lord, if I am quick to criticise. Renew my heart to encourage and support those who serve to build your kingdom. Amen.

ELIZABETH RUNDLE

Accused

They set up false witnesses who said, 'This man never stops saying things against this holy place and the law, for we have heard him say that this Jesus of Nazareth will destroy this place and will change the customs that Moses handed on to us.' And all who sat in the council looked intently at him, and they saw that his face was like the face of an angel.

The 'they' in this passage were influential men representing the synagogue of the Freedmen from countries around the Mediterranean: Cyrene, Alexandria (in Egypt), Cilicia and Asia. The holy city of Jerusalem was a cosmopolitan hub for all Jews. These men were outraged by Stephen's preaching.

Stephen was an educated and gifted preacher, but when he coupled together Jesus and the destruction of the holy temple, to their ears it was heresy at best and, at worst, blasphemy. We can understand their position; the laws of Moses laid down the death penalty for blasphemy (see Leviticus 24). Yet they had missed the point.

The accusation against Stephen strongly suggests that he had been in the temple when Jesus drove out the traders and money-changers and heard him say, 'Destroy this temple, and in three days I will raise it up' (John 2:19). Those who accused Jesus did not understand that he had not said he would destroy the temple in Jerusalem. Jesus had been referring to his own body as a temple, which would be destroyed on the cross and raised in glory on the third day. False witnesses accused Jesus of blasphemy when, at the time, only the Roman powers could put a man to death. Tempers boiled over. Stephen's fate was sealed.

Before we go further with Stephen's story, we need to understand the significance of angels in biblical times. Forget artistic depictions of sweet cherubs suspended on the whitest of wings; biblical angels were seen as direct messengers from God. What do you imagine those accusers saw in Stephen's face? Did his radiant faith unnerve them? He could not be defeated by argument or false witnesses. Neither could the vindictive intent of a mock trial make Stephen crumble. Whose face radiates faith to you?

Lord, thank you for 'angels' who have guided, strengthened and loved me on my faith journey. Amen.

ELIZABETH RUNDLE

The longest 'sermon'

'You stiff-necked people, uncircumcised in heart and ears, you are for-ever opposing the Holy Spirit, just as your ancestors used to do. Which of the prophets did your ancestors not persecute? They killed those who foretold the coming of the Righteous One, and now you have become his betrayers and murderers. You are the ones that received the law as ordained by angels, and yet you have not kept it.'

A friend's five-year-old son sat amazingly still on the wooden pew cuddling his teddy. From the pulpit came a long and winding prayer. When he heard the preacher's 'Amen', the little boy turned to his mother and with a loud stage whisper said, 'That's the longest prayer I've ever heard in my whole life!' We stifled our amusement.

Stephen's defence before the council is indeed the longest recorded 'sermon' in the Bible, a tour de force of all the towering fathers of faith in Hebrew scripture: Abraham, Joseph, Moses and David. Stephen related how, throughout their history, God had raised up prophets to lead the people back into the covenant relationship first bestowed on Abraham. Stephen proceeded to itemise how those great men had been consistently rejected.

Foremost of these national heroes was Moses, who defied Pharaoh to lead the Israelite slaves from Egypt to freedom only to be bombarded with discontent: 'Who made you a ruler and a judge?' (Acts 7:35).

As if the truth about Israel's multiple rejections of God's covenant was not scandalous enough, Stephen hits them with a second revelation: 'The Most High does not dwell in houses made by human hands' (v. 48). At that time the religious leaders believed God inhabited the temple in Jerusalem, whereas Stephen preached that no human creation could contain the almighty creator God. God cannot be owned nor confined. God is.

That mystery and miracle is beyond understanding, but it can be humbly embraced by faith. So, think about places where you feel closer to God, perhaps a church, a cathedral or maybe a mountain or seashore.

Think about those 'thin places' where you glimpse or feel the glory of God.
'The earth will be filled with the knowledge of the glory of the Lord, as the
waters cover the sea' (Habakkuk 2:14).

ELIZABETH RUNDLE

The lynch mob

When they had heard these things, they became enraged and ground their teeth at Stephen. But filled with the Holy Spirit, he gazed into heaven and saw the glory of God and Jesus standing at the right hand of God. 'Look', he said, 'I see the heavens opened and the Son of Man standing at the right hand of God!' But they covered their ears , and with a loud shout all rushed together against him. Then they dragged him out of the city and began to stone him.

There is a gate in Jerusalem's old city walls that opens eastward and from where one can look over to the Mount of Olives. Through this gate shepherds would bring their sheep for sacrifice in the temple, and therefore it was (and still is) known as The Sheep Gate. On the steep slope below this gate you find a small Greek Orthodox Church dedicated to the first Christian martyr, Stephen. So as well as being called The Sheep Gate, for Christian pilgrims this is St Stephen's Gate. This area has always bustled with traders, farmers, tourists, artisans and pilgrims. Then on one fateful day the noise of commerce was drowned by a roaring crowd and the crash of stones. Maybe just feet away from the old city gate, a lynch mob committed a violent murder.

Stephen's inflammatory monologue ended as he declared his accusers had rejected and murdered God's promised Messiah. It was a truth too terrible for them to hear. Then Stephen's gaze lifted above the crowd to the sky. He could 'see' Jesus. To the men who had heard his condemnatory sermon, Stephen was no visionary but a mad blasphemer. He had to be silenced. Luke's account throbs with tension, as the mob violence quickly takes over. Still today, there are a few countries where stoning is a form of capital punishment.

Think about the similarity between Stephen's vision and the account of Jesus' baptism, where the heavens opened. The prophet Ezekiel also visualised the heavens opened to reveal the presence of God (Ezekiel 1:1). For Stephen and the first Christians, it was the ultimate affirmation of God's presence and approval.

Lord, I pray for Christians persecuted for their faith today. Amen.

ELIZABETH RUNDLE

Into all the world

While they were stoning Stephen, he prayed, 'Lord Jesus, receive my spirit.' Then he knelt down and cried in a loud voice, 'Lord, do not hold this sin against them.' When he had said this, he died. And Saul approved of their killing him. That day a severe persecution began against the church in Jerusalem, and all except the apostles were scattered throughout the countryside of Judea and Samaria. Devout men buried Stephen and made loud lamentation over him.

Oh, the skill of God-inspired biblical writers. In a few short verses we have no less than five major strands to think about.

First, prayer. In the extremity of his suffering, Stephen prayed to his Lord. What is prayer but that invisible process which strengthens us with a power beyond understanding?

Second, looking at his two recorded prayers, we cannot escape the similarity with the final prayers of Jesus himself (see Luke 23:34, 46). Like Jesus, Stephen endured a horrendously violent death. A victim of stoning would be fortunate to be knocked unconscious before further stones bludgeoned life from their body. The hallmark of Jesus' life and death was forgiveness.

Third, we have the first mention of Saul (7:58; 8:1), a consenting witness to Stephen's death. Little did Saul imagine he would, one day, be confronted by a vision of Jesus.

Fourth, from that moment, the group of believers in the risen Lord Jesus became victims of 'severe persecution'. Those who publicly professed Jesus as Lord risked everything – home, family and their lives. However, their persecution had an unforeseen effect. The good news of Jesus spread out from Jerusalem, and it is still spreading as you read this.

Finally, Stephen's poignant burial by grieving fellow believers: they also risked everything to give their beloved deacon a fitting funeral.

Stephen's earthly life ended, but the message has no end. Consider how his death was the launch pad to the exciting, groundbreaking new era. The message of salvation through Jesus Christ was spread first by word of mouth, then by the apostles' letters, on into the Gentile world.

Lord Jesus Christ, I pray for your Spirit to inspire and fill my life. Amen.

ELIZABETH RUNDLE

Winter

Is winter the Cinderella season – that is, the unchosen and the also-ran in the race of favourite seasons? I have friends who prefer spring, summer or autumn, but none, I fear, who will declare for winter. Here and now in early January, you may well feel inclined to agree with them.

Why would anyone choose winter? Unless you live in the tropics, where it must be an altogether mystifying concept, winter usually conjures thoughts of wind and rain, freezing fog, and snow and ice, along with soaring energy bills, isolation for the elderly, short days and long nights. For most of us, gone are the days of waking up to beautiful ice patterns on the inside of our windows or warming our gloves on the single bar electric fire – central heating and thermal vests have done much to mitigate the extreme contrasts of winter. Just how much effect the changing climate patterns will have on our classic four seasons remains to be seen; certainly there seems to be an increasing lack of predictability and at times a blurring of those distinctive qualities of each season. To what extent this is either significant or a good thing is part of a much weightier discussion, well beyond the limits of these notes.

God created cold and heat, summer and winter, hail and snow and every variation known to the Met Office – and, on consideration, declared it all 'good'. There must therefore be good reasons to celebrate winter, and not just because of Christmas, the possibility of skiing or for the value of the negative in highlighting the positive, but because of its own inherent qualities and potential.

True, for most of us, winter no longer involves roasting chestnuts on a blazing log fire or skating on the village pond – those Victorian Christmas cards have a lot to answer for. So perhaps we need to dig a little deeper for that winter treasure.

I would love to imagine that, after reading these notes, you will revise your estimation of winter as the wallflower season, and view her not with dread but anticipation. That may be wildly optimistic, but perhaps you will reckon her at least worth asking for a dance or two.

SHEILA WALKER

The promise of winter

Noah built an altar to the Lord and took of every clean animal and of every clean bird and offered burnt offerings on the altar. And when the Lord smelled the pleasing odor, the Lord said in his heart, 'I will never again curse the ground because of humans, for the inclination of the human heart is evil from youth; nor will I ever again destroy every living creature as I have done. As long as the earth endures, seedtime and harvest, cold and heat, summer and winter, day and night, shall not cease.'

As we read this passage we recall that Noah had just endured a most unseasonal time of prolonged rain and flood as God chose to judge wayward humanity by disrupting the meteorological balance. The fact that he promises never to repeat that particular form of judgement suggests that such balance is necessary if plant, animal and human life are to flourish. It is true that some parts of the world suffer from more pronounced seasons of monsoon or drought; maybe this is one of the consequences of the fallenness of all creation, seemingly unfairly challenging some more than others. Sometimes, though, it is our lack of environmental awareness and selfishness which add to the problems, and the remedy is in our own hands. At other times, we can only look to God's mercy and sustaining power and trust that he is indeed at work to redeem and bless.

Balance: hot and cold, summer and winter, day and night. If winter is part of God's promise, the implication is surely that it is not simply to be endured but appreciated and valued. It is a gift, not a punishment; provision, not deprivation. This may not be our first thought on yet another grey sleety day, when the temptation is to echo the cynic who said, 'There are two seasons in Scotland: June and winter.'

Remembering the goodness and wisdom of God, however, is a good antidote – and perhaps rebuke – to cynicism and gloom. His promises are to be received as a lifeline, drawing us to a place of safety and truth.

Faithful God, we read that you are not human being, that you should lie, or a mortal, that you should change your mind (Numbers 23:19). Please help us to discern all that is good in your promise of winter. Amen.

SHEILA WALKER

The why of winter

For to the snow he says, 'Fall on the earth'; and the shower of rain, his heavy shower of rain, serves as a sign on everyone's hand, so that all whom he has made may know it… By the breath of God ice is given, and the broad waters are frozen fast. He loads the thick cloud with moisture; the clouds scatter his lightning. They turn round and round by his guidance, to accomplish all that he commands them on the face of the habitable world. Whether for correction or for his land or for love, he causes it to happen.

One of the hardest and most unsettling things for us, especially in tough times, is the unanswered – and often unanswerable – question 'Why?' We can often cope with all kinds of trials and challenges if it is possible to discern some kind of meaning in it all, or at least some kind of positive spin-off; but it is so much worse when there is not even a glimpse of any silver lining to those clouds. This was a significant part of Job's suffering: it all appeared so undeserved, unproductive and pointless.

The verses above form part of Elihu's challenge to Job. He is the fourth and youngest of Job's 'friends', but his words arguably reflect a deeper view of sin, especially spiritual pride, and a stronger emphasis on suffering as a discipline to bring us to a wiser way of life. Hence the remarkable statement in verse 13 that all that God does, including the worst of winter weather, in whatever way we may interpret it, is either out of discipline or mercy, for people or for the created world they inhabit and are called to steward.

It is not a simple equation. Jesus is quite clear that any particular suffering is not necessarily related to our particular sin, but in some – at times mysterious! – way for the glory of God. While it may therefore be irrelevant for us to ask, 'What have I done to deserve this?', it is important to understand the difference between punishment and discipline. Any form of hardship or suffering can, through the grace of God, deepen our dependence on him, our experience of his faithfulness and our compassion for others.

If indeed he is love, then surely he intends all our winters to bring blessing.

Loving God, may we not rail against our winters but seek to understand how you are at work in and through them. Amen.

SHEILA WALKER

The limits of winter

Yet God my King is from of old, working salvation in the earth. You divided the sea by your might; you broke the heads of the dragons in the waters. You crushed the heads of Leviathan; you gave him as food for the creatures of the wilderness. You cut openings for springs and torrents; you dried up ever-flowing streams. Yours is the day, yours also the night; you established the luminaries and the sun. You have fixed all the bounds of the earth; you made summer and winter.

These verses form part of a plea for help for the nation. The first eleven verses of the psalm lament the humiliation visited on Israel by their enemies and the fact that God appears to have abandoned them. Then comes this reminder of his sovereignty, recognising that both good and apparent evil may come from his hand: fresh water and dried-up rivers; darkness and light; summer and winter. His purpose, though, is to work salvation in the earth, and to that end we can be reassured that he has 'fixed all the bounds of the earth'. Each 'season' has its limits, established by an all-wise and all-powerful God.

We seem to be facing an unquestionably challenging 'season' at present. In recent years it is all about melting ice-caps, meteorological extremes, rising energy prices, ongoing international disputes and often an increasing feeling of powerlessness in the face of a frustrating – what some might call Kafkaesque – absence of any logic or even common sense. On an individual level, too, have we not all experienced times when our cry is 'How long, Lord? How much more can I cope with?'

At such times, we can hold on to God's assurance that he has set boundaries. Though the world may appear to be spiralling out of control, there are limits to this, thanks to the one who remains sovereign, despite the astonishing degree of autonomy he allows us, his creatures, to learn – or not – from our mistakes.

Sovereign Lord, truly you are at work in all things. Nothing takes you by surprise, and no situation is beyond your ability to redeem and renew. Alleluia!

SHEILA WALKER

The enduring of winter

'Pray that your flight may not be in winter or on a Sabbath. For at that time there will be great suffering, such as has not been from the beginning of the world until now, no, and never will be. And if those days had not been cut short, no one would be saved, but for the sake of the elect those days will be cut short.'

In response to his disciples' questioning, Jesus speaks prophetically here of the terrible siege of Jerusalem prior to its fall in AD70. In the event, the siege lasted almost four years; more than a million Jews died and the historian Josephus records that more than 97,000 were taken into captivity before the Romans finally reduced the magnificent temple to ruins and the city to rubble. Appalling though the suffering would be, there was to be no preventing it: no last-minute reprieve as for the citizens of Nineveh when Jonah finally arrived. Some suffering is unavoidable, even under the government of a merciful, sovereign God.

Yet this is not the last word on the subject. Just as the Jews here are urged to pray for mitigating circumstances – that their flight will not be hampered by weather or the restrictions of the sabbath – so it is in our own times of trial we can also know real encouragement. I have often found that, while God does not remove the circumstance or answer the big question, he nevertheless does provide that strength to endure: in the form of a timely friend, a financial gift, a babysitter, a change of medication, a hug. It's as though he is saying, 'It's all right, I am still here and I do understand; some suffering, yes, you must accept but I will walk through these times with you.'

It can be hard to know how to pray, caught between the need to be willing to accept from God both good times and bad, and the instinct, need and encouragement to ask for some relief. Sometimes we can only hold our situation before God and wait, remaining open to receive whatever he may send and asking for grace to discern his gifts, great or small.

In acceptance lies peace: so be it, Lord. Amen.

SHEILA WALKER

The temptation of winter

We are afflicted in every way but not crushed, perplexed but not driven to despair, persecuted but not forsaken, struck down but not destroyed, always carrying around in the body the death of Jesus, so that the life of Jesus may also be made visible in our bodies. For we who are living are always being handed over to death for Jesus' sake, so that the life of Jesus may also be made visible in our mortal flesh.

Hard times, whether poverty, ill health or any other wintry circumstance, bring with them their own temptations. They can steal our joy, our energy, our confidence and our trust in God. We are perplexed, disappointed and disillusioned that God could allow such things to happen to us when we have been doing our best to be faithful followers. Such responses are totally understandable. But we have only to look at the apostle Paul to find an alternative, astonishing response. Later, in 2 Corinthians 11, he lists some of the 'winter' experiences he has had: floggings, shipwrecks, stoning, hunger, dangers and persecutions of all kinds. It is truly amazing that he survived, let alone with the strength or enthusiasm to preach!

What was his secret? No secret, for he tells them openly that he is content to be in places of weakness, because God has told him 'My grace is sufficient for you, for power is made perfect in weakness' (2 Corinthians 12:9). Rather than give in to the temptation to rail at our circumstances and at the God who has allowed them, we are to welcome them as opportunities to prove his power and faithfulness as we are made to realise again how dependent we are on him. Sadly, it is often only when we come to the end of our own resources that we think to cry out for help: when things are going smoothly, the temptation is to treat God, in practice at least, as an optional extra.

Faced with an extreme 'winter', Job's wife encouraged him to 'curse God and die'. Gracious God, save us from falling into despair, doubt or defeat when times are hard, but to hold on with trust and patience, knowing that you are holding us and will not let us go. Amen.

SHEILA WALKER

The possibilities of winter

I will visit you after passing through Macedonia – for I intend to pass through Macedonia – and perhaps I will stay with you or even spend the winter, so that you may send me on my way, wherever I go. I do not want to see you now just in passing, for I hope to spend some time with you, if the Lord permits.

As the writer of Ecclesiastes points out, there is a time for every purpose under heaven. Winter is not the time (at least in the UK) for al fresco breakfasts, planting out seedlings or, in more serious vein, embarking on major military or other campaigns. Despite his restless energy and urgent desire to spread the good news of Jesus, Paul is therefore intending to spend the winter at Corinth, waiting until the bad weather has passed and ships can sail again. Then the Corinthian Christians can speed him on his apostolic way.

From what we know of Paul, though, we can be sure he will not have wasted that winter season. Winter may have its limitations, but it also presents other opportunities. Whereas spring, summer and autumn may tempt us to all kinds of activity, travel or exploration, winter may offer 'down time'. Those long dark winter evenings dreaded by many people may prove an ideal time to recoup, reflect, investigate a new hobby, read and pray. Also, yes, attend to all the paperwork, unfinished knitting, phone calls and some of those annoying household DIY jobs: don't groan – there follows, after all, a real sense of satisfaction, and often some pleasant surprises along the way!

Long winter evenings may also mean more time at home with family. This may be a precious gift or, if we are honest, something of a challenge. We may need to pray for the Holy Spirit's inspiration for ways to reconnect with a teenager, encourage an ailing parent or deepen a relationship with a partner. May we not resent these times, nor even simply occupy them, but draw from them every possible advantage.

Gracious God, help us to realise the potential of this winter season, and be open to the Spirit's leading, that we may deepen our relationship with you and with those around us. Amen.

SHEILA WALKER

The enjoyment of winter

**A woman of strength who can find? She is far more precious than jewels…
She opens her hand to the poor and reaches out her hands to the needy.
She is not afraid for her household when it snows, for all her household
are clothed in crimson. She makes herself coverings; her clothing is fine
linen and purple. Her husband is known in the city gates, taking his seat
among the elders of the land. She makes linen garments and sells them;
she supplies the merchant with sashes. Strength and dignity are her
clothing, and she laughs at the time to come.**

Winter brings challenges: weather, energy bills, ill health, isolation. In his
ode to a capable wife, the writer of Proverbs praises her for her foresight in
planning ahead for tough times so that when the snow comes, she can not
only look after her family but also continue to support those in greater need.

Some plants prepare for winter by accumulating certain sugars and
amino acids, which act as a kind of antifreeze, lowering the freezing point
of their cell contents for protection when frosts come. Animals, too, may
store food or grow a heavier coat. True, they may also migrate or hibernate,
a luxury most of us do not have! For most of us, winter is a time to draw
on resources we may have put aside 'for a rainy day', trusting that God will
grant us the time and energy to renew them in due course. As William Blake
advised: 'In seed time learn, in harvest teach, in winter enjoy.'

For some the particular enjoyment of winter may be the skiing holiday,
but for most, as Edith Sitwell thought, 'Winter is the time for comfort,
for good food and warmth, for the touch of a friendly hand and for a talk
beside the fire: it is the time for home.' A warm scarf, a brisk walk followed
by hot soup, candlelight – these are small things which bring pleasures
distinctive of winter.

Enjoyment is so often dependent on our attitude, and we can choose
to focus on those things which delight rather than disturb us. Sharing that
delight with others enhances it, for us and for them.

---

*Lord, help me to take delight in this season of winter. Surprise me again
with its special gifts. Amen.*

SHEILA WALKER

The necessity of winter

Then the angel showed me the river of the water of life, bright as crystal, flowing from the throne of God and of the Lamb through the middle of the street of the city. On either side of the river is the tree of life with its twelve kinds of fruit, producing its fruit each month, and the leaves of the tree are for the healing of the nations.

In this heavenly kingdom, every season is productive, every month is fruitful. True, this is heaven – but we are granted glimpses of that glory now! For all sorts of reasons, we need winter. For example, some plants need shorter days and lower temperatures to become dormant and store up energy; there are fewer insects; people apparently think more clearly in winter and also sleep better; and because of the earth's alignment, it must be winter somewhere in order for it to be summer somewhere else!

Winter can be beautiful, although as Aristotle told us, to appreciate the beauty of a snowflake it is necessary to stand out in the cold. Cold, though, can be health-giving: Robert Baden-Powell, of scouting fame, slept outdoors in winter as well as summer and said that he only felt seedy when he had been indoors a lot, and that he only caught a cold when he slept in a room. To wake up one morning to the revelation of our surroundings revealed in the black and white of an early snowdrift lends a whole new perspective.

The challenges of life develop and hone our character, when we discover not only the hidden strengths we may have deep within us and the kindness of friends, family, and even strangers, but also the nearness of a loving God and his grace, sufficient for all our need.

The French writer Albert Camus, though not a Christian, said that it was in the depth of winter that he finally learned that there was in him 'an invincible summer'. How much more heartening a discovery might it be for those who enjoy the immeasurable privilege of God's Holy Spirit dwelling in them, bringing light, warmth and encouragement to the darkest of days, literally and metaphorically.

May it be so, Lord. Amen.

SHEILA WALKER

The revelation of winter

He made darkness his covering around him, his canopy thick clouds dark with water. Out of the brightness before him there broke through his clouds hailstones and coals of fire. The Lord also thundered in the heavens, and the Most High uttered his voice. And he sent out his arrows and scattered them; he flashed forth lightnings and routed them. Then the channels of the sea were seen, and the foundations of the world were laid bare at your rebuke, O Lord, at the blast of the breath of your nostrils.

Much as I love the spring and autumn leafiness, there is something especially striking about the bare branches of winter. No longer is there any possibility of concealment: the underlying structures are laid bare, for better or worse. The patterns of dark branches against a pale winter sky have a beauty all of their own, and there is something about their simplicity that refreshes the soul. Just as so many demands and distractions can prevent us from seeing our way clearly, so also can the sight of those unadorned branches remind us to clear a space to check our foundations: that they remain strong and healthy, able to support all that we seek to build on them.

Sometimes God may strip away our protective coverings, as the psalmist writes; this can be painful, if salutary, and maybe there are times when we need such drastic treatment. But every year, winter reminds us that an annual stock take is no bad thing. The American artist Andrew Wyeth comments that he prefers winter, when you feel the bone structure of the landscape, its loneliness, the fact that something waits beneath it, that the whole story doesn't show. The soul of a place is more apparent in winter; perhaps ours, too. There is an honesty, challenging but necessary and restorative.

Until recently, many would argue that the underlying basis of many people's lives, acknowledged or not, was Christian, simply because of our Christian heritage in much of the west. Today, though, our foundations appear shaky. As the concept of 'truth' is challenged, decisions are increasingly made on the basis of circumstance, convenience or who shouts loudest; the branches are in danger of rotting as Christian roots wither.

Lord, give us courage to face honestly what we are basing our lives on, and the desire and humility to respond to all you reveal to us. Amen.

SHEILA WALKER

23

The sobering of winter

No one can lay any foundation other than the one that has been laid; that foundation is Jesus Christ. Now if anyone builds on the foundation with gold, silver, precious stones, wood, hay, straw – the work of each builder will become visible, for the day will disclose it, because it will be revealed with fire, and the fire will test what sort of work each has done. If the work that someone has built on the foundation survives, the builder will receive a wage. If the work is burned up, the builder will suffer loss; the builder will be saved, but only as through fire.

The bare branches of winter may suggest an annual baring of the soul, and here we see that Paul echoes this thought. He reminds us that one day, the Day of Judgement, nothing will remain hidden; so it is salutary for us to check the state of our affairs and our conscience now. On what is my life founded? Is it truly founded on Jesus Christ himself? And how have I built on that foundation, how have I used my God-given talents, how have I made my choices, how have I responded to the needs and opportunities around me? How far has the life and light of Jesus been expressed through me?

Though this may appear a painful prospect, it is perhaps astringent. Putting antiseptic on a wound will sting, but it is the only way to bring true healing. Nor is it a cause for despair if the Holy Spirit convicts us of any neglect, failure or self-interest, for he convicts only to prompt us to seek forgiveness, and that is freely offered. The sacrificial death of Jesus covers every sin, and his resurrection offers new life, as many new beginnings as we need to make him more truly Lord and King.

Pietro Aretino, the 16th-century Italian poet and satirist – and black-mailer – wrote, 'Let us love winter, for it is the spring of genius.' As with life in general, what we derive from it will largely depend on what we bring to it, not so much in terms of gifts and talents but attitude.

Lord Jesus, may we always look for the best, capitalise on whatever opportunities are present, make the most of what is and be open to all that the Holy Spirit can work in and through us – perhaps even 'genius'! So be it, Lord. Amen.

SHEILA WALKER

The cooling off of winter

'Then many will fall away, and they will betray one another and hate one another. And many false prophets will arise and lead many astray. And because of the increase of lawlessness, the love of many will grow cold. But the one who endures to the end will be saved. And this good news of the kingdom will be proclaimed throughout the world, as a testimony to all the nations, and then the end will come.'

Do we want the good news or the bad news? Jesus gives us the bad news first: such will be the disintegration of our culture that our faith will cease to fire us; it will become wintry. Why should this be? What is the connection between lawlessness and loss of a living faith? And what does such a chilled faith look like?

The more we become aware of the erosion of both our environment and our Christian values as a result of governments' action or inaction, the harder it is for us to hold on to our belief in the sovereignty of God and that he is truly at work in all circumstances. Where is he when forests are decimated and individual rights trump social cohesion? When poverty denies potential and peace is forever elusive?

Yet hold on we must, for our belief is true, despite the grimness of the picture continually presented to us by the media. This picture may also be true, but we know that the story is not yet over and that we are told, and need to tell, a different story.

It is understandable that faith can grow weary and become chilled. Where we should be warm and welcoming, we can be cool and exclusive. When we should be outgoing and ready to share, we can be defensive and non-committal. Where we should be open-hearted and ready to listen, we can be legalistic, strident and Pharisaic. Where this is happening, no wonder people do not flock to church; they look for bread, but are offered only stone.

The good news is that there will be those whose faith endures, and nothing can prevent the gospel being preached, one way or another, by you if not by me. Our God is invincible and will always find ways and coworkers for his kingdom to come on earth.

Lord, may we be your coworkers here on earth. Amen.

SHEILA WALKER

The turning of winter

Therefore I will judge you, O house of Israel, all of you according to your ways, says the Lord God. Repent and turn from all your transgressions; otherwise iniquity will be your ruin. Cast away from you all the transgressions that you have committed against me, and get yourselves a new heart and a new spirit! Why will you die, O house of Israel? For I have no pleasure in the death of anyone, says the Lord God. Turn, then, and live.

Although these words of Ezekiel are addressed to the nation of Israel, the context is that his people are being judged not for the sins of their ancestors, but for their own; everyone is responsible for their own choices and behaviour. The command to 'turn' can therefore be seen as both corporate and individual.

In polar and temperate climes, winter is the coldest season; it occurs when a hemisphere is oriented away from the sun. In like manner, the winter of our faith occurs when we are no longer oriented towards the 'sun of righteousness' (Malachi 4:2) – this phrase being understood as referring prophetically to Jesus.

Orienteering is the crossing of unknown land with the aid of a map and a compass. This is not a bad description of our life's journey, although we are not to see that journey as a race, and sadly many today seem to lack the map and compass. For Christians though, the map and compass are a given: our map is the Bible and the wisdom of fellow believers, and our compass is to be set to Jesus and kept from wavering by the leading of the Holy Spirit.

The heartwarming, winter-warming truth is that it is always possible to turn back to God, to reset our compass. It is called repentance and, as John Monsell's epiphany hymn puts it, God will always accept us and 'mornings of joy give for evenings of tearfulness, trust for our trembling and hope for our fear'.

Lord Jesus, keep my compass steady, fixed on you. Amen.

SHEILA WALKER

The warming of winter

A word fitly spoken is like apples of gold in a setting of silver. Like a gold ring or an ornament of gold is a wise rebuke to a listening ear. Like the cold of snow in the time of harvest are faithful messengers to those who send them; they refresh the spirit of their masters. Like clouds and wind without rain is one who boasts of a gift never given. With patience a ruler may be persuaded, and a soft tongue can break bones.

If our faith can become wintry, how can we fan the flame and feed those dying embers? Surely no one wants snow at harvest time? How can this be considered a good thing? But perhaps a wise friend, a faithful messenger, seeing that we are going through a cold spell, will dare to encourage us not simply to look for some kind of 'comfort food' but to take an honest look at ourselves and ask what God is saying to us. What has distracted us, led us to doubt? Have we neglected to feed our faith, or chosen to ignore the teaching or promptings of God? Like the driver who is lost but won't seek directions, it is no good simply ploughing on. The voice that says 'Stop! Check!' is to be heeded, even if some chilly backtracking is involved.

So how might we be that faithful messenger to one another, bringing kindling and matches to reignite a cooling faith? The Russian playwright Anton Chekhov said that people do not notice whether it is winter or summer when they are happy. So, a wise friend will listen. Knowing what is going on, what is troubling the other, what is occupying them, will guide our response and our prayer.

We do not always need to have answers; the willingness to walk alongside, to share and to pray may be all that we can offer. But somehow that is often enough to enable God to heal, restore and fire up. As we resolve to continue to love, to trust and to pray, miracles may happen. A Japanese proverb tells us that 'one kind word can warm three winter months'.

Gracious God, thank you that you can multiply our loaves and fishes to feed a hungry faith. Help us to look out for those who especially need our encouragement and love. Amen.

SHEILA WALKER

The poetry of winter

For as the rain and the snow come down from heaven and do not return there until they have watered the earth, making it bring forth and sprout, giving seed to the sower and bread to the eater, so shall my word be that goes out from my mouth; it shall not return to me empty, but it shall accomplish that which I purpose, and succeed in the thing for which I sent it.

Isaiah's words imply that God's seasons are every bit as necessary and productive as his words, containing the potential for growth and fruitfulness. The 13th-century Persian poet Rumi wrote the beautiful line: 'I don't think the garden loses its ecstasy in winter. It's quiet, but the roots down there are riotous.'

We are all different – in temperament, circumstances and outlook. Our response to winter will therefore be nuanced, individual, but I would love to think that in some way the Holy Spirit can show how in this 'down' season, our roots can nevertheless be 'riotous'. To be able to reflect the love of Jesus in every season will be a powerful witness to many; by his grace, may we not suffer from seasonal affective disorder and have the discernment to minister to those who do.

The part each of us is called to play in life is unique, as beautiful as a snowflake, and only you can fulfil that calling. Paul told the Christians at Philippi that we are each God's poem, and a poem is a very individual thing. What kind of poem will you write with your life? Perhaps you might reflect on those things you really appreciate about winter: thank God for them, for that special creativity, and pray for opportunities to share your insights, to encourage others who may be less positive. The other side of the coin might be to reflect on the challenges – those you face and those faced by others – and ask God how your poem might speak to theirs.

Elegy or eulogy? There can be a place for both, but it is good to seek to finish on a note of praise and trust in God. Though if all else fails, we can remember another poet, Shelley, who wrote: 'If winter comes, can spring be far behind?'

SHEILA WALKER

Haggai

January seems like a good time to study the book of Haggai, because it is a story about a new beginning, and new beginnings are appropriate at the start of a new year. As the calendar changes, we instinctively feel like turning over a new leaf, and our readings this week will encourage us towards personal spiritual renewal.

Knowing the background to the book is important for understanding its message. The people of Israel had been carried away into exile in Babylon around 597 BC. Then, in 538 BC King Cyrus gave permission for some to return to Jerusalem and rebuild the temple. This they did under the leadership of Zerubbabel (the governor) and Joshua (the high priest). This story is told in the first part of the book of Ezra.

At first things went well. The group enthusiastically rebuilt the altar and began to offer sacrifices again. Then they laid the foundation for the temple building with much rejoicing. But that is where things got stuck. Local people frustrated their plans and complained to the new king in Babylon, Artaxerxes, who called a halt to the work. That led to a standstill and a loss of motivation.

God, however, had other plans. At the same time as a new king, Darius, came to rule in Babylon, God sent two prophets to stir up the people and encourage them to continue building (see Ezra 5:1–2). With the inspiration of Haggai and Zechariah, the people began to build again, and this time Darius supported their efforts, so the work went ahead and prospered (see Ezra 6:14).

Sometimes we feel becalmed in our walk with God. Perhaps circumstances are against us, and discouragement sets in. We lose heart and want to give up. If that describes you, then these readings will be timely, because Haggai's words will encourage you not to give up. And if your walk with God is buoyant and fruitful, there will be much here to strengthen and inspire you to continue serving God and to discover a new vision of what God can do in your church and community. Either way, this year may be the start of something special for you.

TONY HORSFALL

Time to rebuild

In the second year of King Darius, on the first day of the sixth month, the word of the Lord came through the prophet Haggai to Zerubbabel son of Shealtiel, governor of Judah, and to Joshua son of Jozadak, the high priest: This is what the Lord Almighty says: 'These people say, "The time has not yet come to rebuild the Lord's house."' Then the word of the Lord came through the prophet Haggai: 'Is it a time for you yourselves to be living in your panelled houses, while this house remains a ruin?'

It is easy to start a project, but not always easy to finish one. Sometimes we have great ideas and begin our task enthusiastically, but then over time and with the emergence of problems and difficulties, we lose enthusiasm, and the project is left unfinished and neglected. Sadly, that is what happened to the 'Rebuild the temple' project in Jerusalem. They had started but not finished.

At just the right moment – God's timing is always impeccable – God sent Haggai with a message for the two main leaders, Zerubbabel and Joshua. It was a challenging word to stir both leaders and people into action again, shaking them out of their lethargy and re-energising them for work. The gist of it was this: why should God's house be in ruins when you are living in luxurious homes?

When we get discouraged in God's work, the natural response is to focus on ourselves. Personal concerns begin to dominate, and our energies are transferred to our own agendas; the work of God is neglected. That is when we, too, need a wake-up call, something to shake us out of our lethargy and help us reorganise our priorities.

God has many ways of speaking to us and grabbing our attention. The word of God has many ways of finding us out and confronting us in our need. It is important when we hear God's voice to recognise who is speaking and to respond accordingly.

Lord, keep me from complacency. Shake me out of lethargy. Awaken my heart to seek you. Rekindle the flame of love within me. Amen.

TONY HORSFALL

A chastening hand

This is what the Lord Almighty says: 'Give careful thought to your ways. Go up into the mountains and bring down timber and build my house, so that I may take pleasure in it and be honoured,' says the Lord. 'You expected much, but see, it turned out to be little. What you brought home, I blew away. Why?' declares the Lord Almighty. 'Because of my house, which remains a ruin, while each of you is busy with your own house.'

'Sorry, I would love to help, but I'm just too busy.' Perhaps you have heard that excuse. Perhaps you have given it yourself, and maybe it is true – so often we are simply too busy. Life crowds in around us and the demands of work, family, friends and church take over until we feel lost in the maelstrom of activity. And in the turmoil, God is often relegated to the sidelines of our life.

It may be helpful to know that busyness is not just a 21st-century problem. It was one of the root causes of the spiritual malaise that had overtaken God's people on their return to Jerusalem. Now God addresses the issue and asks the people to carefully consider their ways.

Self-examination is not something we are good at on the whole. We shy away from 'navel gazing' and anything that smacks of introspection. As a result, we live on the surface of life and never get to know ourselves properly. God had been speaking to his people, gently chastising them for their neglect of spiritual matters by squeezing them economically, but they missed the message because they were too busy to hear.

God's concern for the temple was not because of the building but because of what it represented – his presence at the heart of the nation. This is what concerns God for us too – God desires to be at the centre of our lives, not the periphery. When God is given his rightful place, life works better and God's blessing flows towards us. God's presence with us is worth more than anything else.

What does it mean for you to 'give careful thought to your ways'?
As you reflect on your life, what adjustments might you need to make?

TONY HORSFALL

The joy of obedience

Then Zerubbabel son of Shealtiel, Joshua son of Jozadak, the high priest, and the whole remnant of the people obeyed the voice of the Lord their God and the message of the prophet Haggai, because the Lord their God had sent him. And the people feared the Lord. Then Haggai, the Lord's messenger, gave this message of the Lord to the people: 'I am with you,' declares the Lord. So the Lord stirred up the spirit of Zerubbabel son of Shealtiel, governor of Judah, and the spirit of Joshua son of Jozadak, the high priest, and the spirit of the whole remnant of the people.

I once heard it said that revival is but the beginning of a new obedience. If that is true – and I believe it is – we can have personal and corporate renewal at any time. All that is needed is for us to obey whatever God is saying to us.

For the people in Jerusalem that meant getting back to work on the temple project. I love the way that Zerubbabel and Joshua lead the people into obedience by setting the example. That, to me, is good leadership. Leaders cannot expect those they lead to go further in following God than they are willing to go themselves. It is incumbent on leaders to be leading the way in responsiveness to God.

To fear God is not to be afraid of him or to cower before him, thinking of him as a bullying tyrant. To fear in this sense is to respect God, to recognise his authority, to be ready to do whatever he asks of us. It is to live in obedience to his rule.

Whenever God's people respond like this to God's word, the sense of his presence among them increases. 'I am with you' is no mere platitude, but the confirmation that the Lord Almighty is delighted with us. The divine presence energises and motivates us. It can be felt, and it changes and transforms us. It is the mark of a company of people keen to do God's will and bring glory to his name.

Perhaps you feel your spirit stirred as you read today. Don't be afraid but give yourself to whatever he is doing within you.

TONY HORSFALL

Be strong, do not fear

'Who of you is left who saw this house in its former glory? How does it look to you now? Does it not seem to you like nothing? But now be strong, Zerubbabel,' declares the Lord. 'Be strong, Joshua son of Jozadak, the high priest. Be strong, all you people of the land,' declares the Lord, 'and work. For I am with you,' declares the Lord Almighty. 'This is what I covenanted with you when you came out of Egypt. And my Spirit remains among you. Do not fear.'

We do not have much biographical information about Haggai. It has been suggested that he was one of those transported to Babylon among the original exiles. If so, then he would be in his 70s, and a reminder to us that God can use us no matter what our age. It also suggests that he would have seen the original temple in its architectural splendour.

Perhaps the builders were comparing the restored temple unfavourably with the original one, and no doubt it could not match the same external beauty. What counts, however, is not striking architecture but the glory of God's presence filling the place. Some of us perhaps worship in cathedrals, splendid churches or modern purpose-built buildings; others will gather in community centres, school halls and even pubs. It is not the building that matters, but who is worshipped there and whether or not God is glorified.

The task before the builders is a daunting one, but God speaks to reassure them. Three times God says, 'Be strong.' He speaks directly to Zerubbabel and Joshua as leaders, and to the people as a whole. They can be strong because God is with them and will fortify them. It is not that they must find strength within themselves, but that God will give them his strength. Any of us might be unnerved if we feel we have to make things happen, but we do not. We simply have to allow God to work through us.

It is the Spirit who makes the connection between divine power and human weakness. As we open ourselves to him, divine life flows into us.

Lord, strengthen me to be the person you want me to be and do the things you have called me to do.

TONY HORSFALL

33

Filled with glory

'This is what the Lord Almighty says: "In a little while I will once more shake the heavens and the earth, the sea and the dry land. I will shake all nations, and what is desired by all nations will come, and I will fill this house with glory," says the Lord Almighty. "The silver is mine and the gold is mine," declares the Lord Almighty. "The glory of this present house will be greater than the glory of the former house," says the Lord Almighty. "And in this place I will grant peace," declares the Lord Almighty.'

Vision is important in accomplishing any task. To persevere with a difficult task, we must have the end in view, to see clearly what we are working towards and why it matters. In rebuilding the temple, the workers can be inspired to know that the glory of God will fill the place even more than the previous one. It may be a humbler building, but it will contain the very presence of God, which is why it will be so special.

Haggai has an exalted view of God. He sees him as the Lord Almighty, the one in control of nations. The world is not governed by royalty, politicians or generals but by God. When he shakes the earth, they tremble and fall. Even proud Babylon was overthrown. Neither are economists or financiers in charge. Silver and gold belong to God, whose wealth is unsurpassable. When God is our provider, we need not fear economic upheaval.

As with many prophetic books, Haggai reaches forward beyond his own era to the coming of Christ. It is likely that 'what is desired by all nations' is a reference to Jesus, who as Saviour of the world will meet the longings and desires of all people. His coming will be the ultimate expression of the glory of God, and his triumphal entry into Jerusalem and the temple the crowning glory of that sacred place.

The one who comes as Prince of Peace will bring peace to all people – peace *with* God through the forgiveness of sins, and the peace *of* God as his gift to keep them steady in times of turmoil.

Lord, let me see your glory and know your peace. Amen.

TONY HORSFALL

I will bless you

'Now give careful thought to this from this day on – consider how things were before one stone was laid on another in the Lord's temple… From this day on, from this twenty-fourth day of the ninth month, give careful thought to the day when the foundation of the Lord's temple was laid. Give careful thought: is there yet any seed left in the barn? Until now, the vine and the fig-tree, the pomegranate and the olive tree have not borne fruit. From this day on I will bless you.'

Some days stand out, don't they? They are turning points in our lives when something happens that changes things forever, and the date is permanently inscribed on our hearts. The temple had not been rebuilt yet, but the people's obedience and response meant that they were no longer under God's discipline. From now on (scholars suggest 18 December, 520 BC) the blessing of God would be upon them.

Once again Haggai urges leaders and people to look back and consider how things were when he first spoke to them. Because of their complacency and inactivity, the chastening hand of God had brought them low through drought and famine, disease and storm. Grain and wine were scarce, fruit crops failed, money went nowhere (1:6, 10–11; 2:16–17, 19). It was a miserable time.

Only when they returned to God did things change. Now, because of their renewed obedience, the discipline has been lifted and they are under the favour of God. Here is a lesson to be taken to heart. Blessing accompanies obedience; discipline follows disobedience. Hopefully they will not walk away from God again.

But what does blessing look like? I would suggest first and foremost it is inwards, a deep sense of peace and well-being, of things being right with God. Love, joy and peace would sum it up. Then, it may be external as well, in the provision of what we need, seeing answers to our prayers and being conscious of God's guidance and providence at work in our lives. Every tangible blessing is a gift from God and should lead to a humble and grateful heart.

Meditate on this: 'From this day on I will bless you.'

TONY HORSFALL

Chosen for purpose

The word of the Lord came to Haggai a second time on the twenty-fourth day of the month: 'Tell Zerubbabel governor of Judah that I am going to shake the heavens and the earth. I will overturn royal thrones and shatter the power of the foreign kingdoms. I will overthrow chariots and their drivers; horses and their riders will fall, each by the sword of his brother. "On that day," declares the Lord Almighty, "I will take you, my servant Zerubbabel son of Shealtiel," declares the Lord, "and I will make you like my signet ring, for I have chosen you," declares the Lord Almighty.'

Some people stand out from the crowd, either because of their appearance, their gifting or their accomplishments. Some stand out because of who they are, their character and their personality. Zerubbabel stands out in many ways, but primarily because he was a godly leader.

One of the first to return from the exile, he stood out as a natural leader and was made governor of Judah. He was not a priest like his friend and colleague Joshua; his role was more political and secular, but he exercised it in a spiritual way. That is much to be admired. He knew what it was to be convicted by God's word and to respond in obedience. His spirit was stirred into action by the knowledge that God was with them.

He is called 'my servant' by God, which shows the depth of his character and genuineness of his walk with God. Godly leaders are first of all servants: they lead not for prestige or power, nor even personal gain, but in order to serve those they lead. They are humble-minded, gentle in their approach and faithful in their calling.

God shares his secrets with his servants, and Zerubbabel is personally told of the shaking that will happen in the political realm. This is to prepare him for what lies ahead. But he is also told of the special part he is to play in the future, and how God will use him, likening him to a signet ring (v. 23). This is a way of saying he would exercise authority on God's behalf, a huge honour.

Pray for godly leaders, so crucial in the renewal of the church.

TONY HORSFALL

If you've enjoyed this set of reflections by **Tony Horsfall**,
check out his books published with BRF, including...

Mentoring Conversations
30 key topics to explore together

978 0 85746 925 0
£9.99

Working from a Place of Rest
*Jesus and the key to
sustaining ministry*

978 0 80039 220 5
£9.99

To order, visit **brfonline.org.uk** or use the order form at the end.

John 5—7

When I read John's gospel, I always imagine the writer as an aged and experienced Christian who has ruminated on years of remembering the words and deeds of Jesus and what it has meant to him as someone seeking to follow him faithfully. In the chapters we will be studying and praying through for the next two weeks, there are many of the themes of this richly layered gospel present: healing, teaching, astounding claims and sayings of Jesus, Old Testament references to water, bread and life, and more. There are words that recur throughout the gospel which have so much more than their surface meaning, such as seeing, coming, believing. They all throw the spotlight on to the person of Jesus and compel us to face up to the two questions that John raises in his prologue: 'Who are you?' and 'What are you looking for?'

John seeks to answer the first question for us by narrating the 'signs' that point to Jesus' identity and by giving accounts of teaching which sometimes speak plainly and at other times employ images that seem mysterious, even obscure, but which are rooted in the scriptures. They draw us in to think for ourselves about God and what he is like, about how he has revealed himself and what it means to relate to him.

Only we can answer the second question about our deepest desires, but in asking it, we are made to reflect on what really matters and how Jesus invites us to find those desires satisfied in him. This mysterious person – who calls us friends and calls us to be with him, who knows God intimately and was with him from the beginning – came and pitched his tent among us so that he could give us life in all its fullness. Yet his invitation to fullness of life caused deep controversy, and we see that building in intensity even in this brief section of the gospel.

As you read words that may be very familiar, ask the Lord to help you see them afresh in all their astounding truth, and hear the Lord himself inviting you to tell him your deepest desires and discover anew that in him all our longings are satisfied.

LIZ HOARE

Beth-zatha

There was a festival of the Jews, and Jesus went up to Jerusalem. Now in Jerusalem by the Sheep Gate there is a pool, called in Hebrew Beth-zatha, which has five porticoes. In these lay many ill, blind, lame, and paralysed people. One man was there who had been ill for thirty-eight years. When Jesus saw him lying there and knew that he had been there a long time, he said to him, 'Do you want to be made well?'

What a strange question to ask a lame person, we might say, and preachers and commentators have speculated widely on the possible reasons. However, Jesus, who possessed profound insight into human nature, asked precisely the right question of this helpless man, whom he knew had been there 'a long time'.

We are not told why Jesus singled him out from among the crowd milling in the porticoes. Notice that Jesus did not say that he could or would heal him in the first instance; he simply asked the man if he wanted to be healed. We need to hear the first question Jesus asked John's disciples – 'What are you looking for?' (1:38) – along with this question, because it is about desire. What had gone on during that 'long time'?

From his reply it would seem that over the years of lying there, he had become wholly at the mercy of his sickness. As the explanation he gave may indicate, he was now identified with his lameness and had given up any hope of being a recipient of the healing that lay in the disturbance of the waters. Anyone who had tried to help him was now gone and he was left alone with his lot.

But now, it was as if everything else: the setting, the other sick people, the helpers and the rest, all fell away as the spotlight fell on this divinely appointed meeting. Jesus came to him in his need, not the other way round and, in the moment, the only thing that mattered was that Jesus had seen him.

You might like to take some time to picture the scene and place yourself in it as the person whom Jesus singles out for attention. What is the question that Jesus asks you that pinpoints your deepest desire? How will you answer his loving gaze?

LIZ HOARE

'Stand up and walk'

The ill man answered him, 'Sir, I have no one to put me into the pool when the water is stirred up, and while I am making my way, someone else steps down ahead of me.' Jesus said to him, 'Stand up, take your mat and walk.' At once the man was made well, and he took up his mat and began to walk.

When people undertake counselling to deal with issues in their lives, a lot of talking is involved on their part, with the counsellor taking on a listening role. The latter's job is to listen well, not only to what is said but also to what remains unsaid. As with the initial information we are given about the sick man at the pool, without hearing him speak, it is easy to speculate about the tone of his response to Jesus' question. Was he whining in a self-pitying way, or was he simply stating the facts?

The pool of Beth-zatha seems to have been sacred to pagans as well as Jews according to archaeological finds at the site, and it was believed by some that the occasional bubbling up of the water was the work of an angel. Its reputed healing powers had not worked for this man, however, despite 38 years of waiting, but the simple command of Jesus to stand up and walk was immediate.

This is the second healing Jesus does in John's gospel and a further 'sign' of who he is, though that is not pointed out here. John includes the healing as a further indication that Jesus is the bringer of life and healing. The Greek word translated as 'Stand up' is the same one regularly used in the New Testament for 'resurrection'. The idea that new life should come out of the waters of chaos echoes the creation story in Genesis, for with a word God created and saw that it was good. Jesus, the Word incarnate, has come and in the mystery of God's ways, one sick individual experiences such new life within himself that he is made well.

As you pray today, try bringing situations of chaos that seem hopeless to God and ask for him to touch them with his resurrection life.

LIZ HOARE

'Carry your mat'

Now that day was a Sabbath. So the Jews said to the man who had been cured, 'It is the Sabbath; it is not lawful for you to carry your mat.' But he answered them, 'The man who made me well said to me, "Take up your mat and walk."' They asked him, 'Who is the man who said to you, "Take it up and walk"?' Now the man who had been healed did not know who it was, for Jesus had disappeared in the crowd that was there.

Jesus frequently got into disputes with the religious leaders of his day over keeping the sabbath. Here the man who was newly healed unwittingly creates a new conflict when he was seen carrying his mat on the sabbath. It seems that he was so shaken by his sudden ability to walk that he neither knew it was the sabbath, nor had he checked out who it was who made him well.

There may be a subtle hint that something was still not right in the phrase 'He did not know who it was' and this is borne out by the subsequent verses that describe another meeting with Jesus and then the way he informed the authorities. It is interesting that when Jesus met him again, the man was in the temple, perhaps to offer thanks to God that he had been healed. If so, there is irony in his failure to see that in Jesus he had met God face to face.

'Who is the man?' is the crucial question for the gospel writer, as it is for all future readers of the text. From the outset, John is clear that Jesus is the Word made flesh, and we are constantly being invited to 'see' and 'believe'. In healing the man Jesus shows himself to be the life-giver. As his teaching about the sabbath will demonstrate, Jesus knew himself to be 'the only Son of the Father', who goes on working to sustain the world, even on the sabbath, over which he is Lord.

How many debates about the sabbath have become sidetracked into arguments about keeping rules? The authorities saw a mat being carried. Jesus had seen the man who would carry it.

Lord, help me to recognise you and worship you in spirit and in truth today. Amen.

LIZ HOARE

'The Son does likewise'

Jesus said to them, 'Very truly, I tell you, the Son can do nothing on his own, but only what he sees the Father doing, for whatever the Father does, the Son does likewise. The Father loves the Son and shows him all that he himself is doing, and he will show him greater works than these, so that you will be astonished. Indeed, just as the Father raises the dead and gives them life, so also the Son gives life to whomever he wishes.'

What a beautiful picture of the intimacy shared between the Father and the Son these verses portray. In explaining that he only does what he sees the Father doing, Jesus reveals the core motivation of his life. He is constantly listening for guidance and direction in his actions so that he keeps in step at every moment with his Father in heaven.

The love between the Father and the Son is such that there are no secrets, no hidden motives or no-go areas. The unity between them is based on love and trust and is utterly transparent. Jesus is not ashamed to be completely dependent on his Father, who in turn shows him everything he is doing.

All this arose out of the healing by Jesus of a man who could not help himself, and the subsequent discomfort of those whose settled views on how the world should be had been upset. Later in this gospel, Jesus will invite his followers to join this intimate circle of Father and Son as those whom he has called 'friends' (15:15). They, and by implication, we, may share this relationship which, as the gospel shows at every point, is life-transforming.

We know from our own experience that where there is love, transformation becomes possible, and without it, our lives are stunted. One of the key things Jesus sees the Father doing is loving, and he in turn gives himself in love.

Make time today to ponder God's love for you and how he shows this to you. As you do this, look for ways to love in turn, telling God in adoration that you receive his love with joy and asking for his strength to love the people he brings across your path and the world in which you are placed.

LIZ HOARE

Love and judgement

'The Father judges no one, but has given all judgement to the Son, so that all may honour the Son just as they honour the Father. Anyone who does not honour the Son does not honour the Father who sent him. Very truly, I tell you, anyone who hears my word and believes him who sent me has eternal life and does not come under judgement but has passed from death to life.'

'Judgement' is one of those Bible words that comes with certain images of God that many people struggle with. God the angry judge, watching out for the slightest deviation from his rules and uttering words of condemnation, are a long way from yesterday's image of intimacy between a father and son. How may we hold love and judgement in tension so that we do not distort the character of God for ourselves and for others?

The person of Jesus is key in our passage today and helps us focus on the wider message of John's gospel. We cannot be content with the limited view of God as distant judge if we take Jesus and his gift of eternal life (v. 24) seriously. It is a gift offered in love, as yesterday's reading reminded us, and it contains such a quality of life as to take us beyond the confines of our experience and imaginations. Even as we ponder this amazing and unwarranted gift, however, we must surely acknowledge that judgement in itself is a good thing, especially for those whose earthly life has been beset by injustice.

In matters of life and death, only the Lord of life can make things new. Since God has entrusted judgement to his Son Jesus, we may have complete confidence that the Lord of all the earth will do what is right (Genesis 18:25). The giver of life, the one who call us friends, and who wants to draw all people to himself is to be trusted in life and in death (John 12:32; 15:15). Because we are created with the freedom to choose, the eternal life Jesus gives comes as we 'hear [his] word and believe' (v. 24).

Lord, help me to hear your invitation to believe, today and always. Amen.

LIZ HOARE

Search the scriptures

'You search the scriptures because you think that in them you have eternal life, and it is they that testify on my behalf. Yet you refuse to come to me to have life. I do not accept glory from humans. But I know that you do not have the love of God in you. I have come in my Father's name, and you do not accept me… If you believed Moses, you would believe me, for he wrote about me. But if you do not believe what he wrote, how will you believe what I say?'

As a young Christian, I followed a series of Bible studies called 'Search the scriptures', which were designed to stimulate my own thinking about the Bible in relation to my life. Over three years they took me through the whole Bible and of course the idea was to continue to read, study and live out the contents of God's word for the rest of my life.

As I learned to read them, I realised that the scriptures did indeed contain the words of eternal life because they led me to Jesus, the living Word. It was obvious in the gospels and the letters of the New Testament, but there he was in the pages of the Old Testament as well (see vv. 46–47). Why, then, could the religious leaders not see that Jesus was speaking the truth about himself and fall down and worship him?

Jesus accuses them of refusing to come to him. Though Jesus came in the name of his Father, the God whom they worshipped, they did not accept him or his claims. No one can be argued into the kingdom of God, though many have tried. But sometimes the veil is so dense that not even the living proof standing before our eyes can break through the hardness of human hearts.

We are presented again with the freedom to choose whether or not to open our hearts to receive Jesus and enter into a relationship with him. The invitation to do so remains, and even for those who accept it, there is always more to discover and grow into.

As we read these words again, may we allow them to challenge us to come to him and find greater depth of understanding of his love for us and what it means to share his life.

LIZ HOARE

God's abundance

'There is a boy here who has five barley loaves and two fish. But what are they among so many people?' Jesus said, 'Make the people sit down.' Now there was a great deal of grass in the place, so they sat down, about five thousand in all. Then Jesus took the loaves, and when he had given thanks he distributed them to those who were seated; so also the fish, as much as they wanted.

It is sometimes said that John 6 replaces the narrative of the last supper recounted by the other three gospels. It contains the feeding of the 5,000 and lengthy discourses about Jesus as the bread of life. The Greek word for 'giving thanks' is *eucharistein* from which we derive the word eucharist, and there are many other words in John 6 that relate to the events of the night before Jesus died, such as eating, drinking, blood, death and eternal life.

Even though the passage above is only a snapshot of the full chapter, there is much to notice and meditate on. We enter the story at the point when a boy's simple lunch becomes the means by which Jesus feeds a multitude. Five loaves (probably very small) and two fish (also probably small) are an almost laughable starting point for a grand miracle, and Andrew is clearly not impressed. But Jesus makes no disparaging comments. He never laughs at our faith, however feeble it seems to us. His gracious arms extend to every paltry act of love and service we have to offer, and he takes what we bring and works wonders with it for the sake of his kingdom.

As with the turning of water into wine at the wedding of Cana (John 2:1–11), there is an emphasis on super-abundance. Even the passing comment about there being a great deal of grass there, emphasises God's generosity through nature. People were able to eat as much as they wanted and there was plenty left over.

But first, Jesus took the loaves and fish and gave thanks to his Father. The crowd that had followed him because they had witnessed the signs he was doing, were now themselves recipients of his generous provision.

Meditate throughout the day on God's abundance of grace in your life.

LIZ HOARE

Turn from temptation

When they were satisfied, he told his disciples, 'Gather up the fragments left over, so that nothing may be lost.' So they gathered them up, and from the fragments of the five barley loaves, left by those who had eaten, they filled twelve baskets. When the people saw the sign that he had done, they began to say, 'This is indeed the prophet who is to come into the world.' When Jesus realised that they were about to come and take him by force to make him king, he withdrew again to the mountain by himself.

Who is this man who performs miracles and teaches with such authority? Is he the long-awaited prophet? Someone who could be made king who would lead them to freedom from the hated Roman occupiers?

Since it was Passover (see John 6:4), the connection between prophet, king and the 'sign' of the feeding of the 5,000 is no accident. The writer is pointing us to Moses, who was both a prophet and the leader of the people and who had fed the escaping enslaved nation with heavenly manna (Exodus 16).

The crowd's idea of making Jesus king was focused entirely in this world. Before we condemn them, remember that they were an occupied people who had suffered defeat and humiliation from Rome. Here was someone who could lead an insurrection and gain freedom for Israel. This was as far as the imagination of the crowd could go at this point, but there is a deep irony at work which the author wants us to grasp. Jesus was indeed a king, only not of this world.

Was Jesus tempted by the prospect of being given power to lead a revolt against Rome and gain glory through it? It is difficult not to recall the temptations in the wilderness when Satan showed him all the kingdoms of the world and offered them to Jesus if only he would bow down and worship him (Matthew 4:1–11). Yet the one who did only what he saw his Father doing was intimate with a higher authority and knew that this was not God's way. So he did the only thing anyone can do with temptation: he 'withdrew'.

Staying close to God and turning away from temptation is the only way to escape its lure for us too.

'Do not bring us to the time of trial, but rescue us from the evil one'
(Matthew 6:13).

LIZ HOARE

'It is I, do not be afraid'

When evening came, his disciples went down to the sea, got into a boat and started across the sea to Capernaum. It was now dark, and Jesus had not yet come to them. The sea became rough because a strong wind was blowing. When they had rowed about three or four miles, they saw Jesus walking on the sea and coming near the boat, and they were terrified. But he said to them, 'It is I; do not be afraid.'

This story has brought comfort to countless people who have been wracked by fear. It is worth noting that comfort was not the first reaction of the disciples here. A rough sea and then a ghostly figure walking on the water was nothing less than terrifying, even though it seems they recognised him early on.

The passage is deeply theological as well as being an invitation to pray and meditate on the presence of the Lord in the storms of our lives. In the Old Testament there are references to God's power over the sea, which was a symbol of chaos to Israel. Only God controls the waves of the sea. Jesus' words to his disciples could be taken at face value, for in Greek *'ego eimi'* could simply mean 'It's me.' They could also point to God's revelation of himself in Exodus, 'I am', and echo other passages in John where Jesus identifies himself with God by using these words (e.g. John 4:26). This 'sign', then, like all the others in John, is about who Jesus is.

Furthermore, the incident shows how Jesus is free to come and go, something that will be much more evident after the resurrection, and something that we experience in a sense in our daily lives. Sometimes the Lord seems so close and we feel his presence, while at other times, he seems far away, absent, even. Yet God never leaves us alone, even though it might seem to be so. He wants us to hear his words: 'It is I; do not be afraid.' He also wants us, like the disciples who desired to receive him into their boat, to desire to receive him more deeply into our hearts and lives.

Help me to know your presence close by today, Lord. Amen.

LIZ HOARE

Feeding on the bread of life

Then Jesus said to them, 'Very truly, I tell you, it was not Moses who gave you the bread from heaven, but it is my Father who gives you the true bread from heaven. For the bread of God is that which comes down from heaven and gives life to the world.' They said to him, 'Sir, give us this bread always.' Jesus said to them, 'I am the bread of life. Whoever comes to me will never be hungry, and whoever believes in me shall never be thirsty.'

One of the characteristics of a Christian is that our desires change, sometimes abruptly, sometimes over a long period of time. This happens as we grow closer to God and learn to want what he wants for us, so that we bear witness to his likeness in the world. In our passage today, the crowd wants to have bread that will satisfy their human craving for food, but as Jesus reminded Satan in the wilderness, human beings cannot live by bread alone (Matthew 4:4). We need food that satisfies the soul, and Jesus offers this freely from his own being when he says, 'I am the bread of life.'

John has already covered the encounter with the woman of Samaria, who moved from her desire to be free of having to collect water from the well every day to the excited discovery that Jesus could satisfy her spiritual needs (see John 4, especially vv. 14–15, 28–29). John links the bread of life closely to the invitation to 'believe' in Jesus and trust him (6:29).

Notice, first, that Jesus emphasises that it is his Father in heaven who gives the true bread, and then Jesus uses the phrase '*ego eimi*' again, which so enraged his opponents because they knew he was implying that he was divine. Just as God fed the people in the wilderness, Jesus also feeds those who come to him.

Second, ponder the extravagance of Jesus' statement that 'anyone' who comes to him will never be hungry or thirsty again. It is an invitation that we may 'taste and see' for ourselves. Not all will take up the invitation, and why that should be so is a mystery, but having done so, we have no need to search anywhere else for satisfaction.

What does it mean for you to feed on the bread of life?

LIZ HOARE

Open invitation

Everything that the Father gives me will come to me, and anyone who comes to me I will never drive away, for I have come down from heaven not to do my own will but the will of him who sent me. And this is the will of him who sent me, that I should lose nothing of all that he has given me but raise it up on the last day.

As we saw in yesterday's reading, Jesus offers an open invitation to come to him, but compels no one to believe. The promise in today's reading is a wonderful reassuring word to anyone who has cried out to God and wondered if in fact God heard or maybe they were somehow excluded from God's mercy. Jesus is emphatic that he will never turn away anyone who comes to him. In this, he is following the will of his heavenly Father, because he came to do his will.

There is a wonderful detail in the feeding of the 5,000 that Jesus told his disciples to gather up the fragments 'so that nothing may be lost' (6:12). Nothing is overlooked or wasted in God's economy. Yesterday we pondered human desire, and today we see God's desire for his world. God's will is that nothing should be lost. There is an echo here of the good shepherd who goes out to look for the one sheep that is lost, even though he has 99 others safely enclosed in the sheepfold.

Jesus longs for us to come to him and place our trust in him. During his life he healed people, taught them about his heavenly Father and set an example of a life that was truth incarnate. Yet even though he was such an attractive human being, he still suffered rejection and eventual death at the hands of his enemies. Before he raises us up on the last day, he was put to death and had to be raised up by his heavenly Father. Implied in these verses is the truth that God is always the one to take the initiative. He cannot be manipulated, and there is great freedom in that for us to come to him.

Thank God for his generous, self-giving love.

LIZ HOARE

Having the words of eternal life

Because of this many of his disciples turned back and no longer went about with him. So Jesus asked the twelve, 'Do you also wish to go away?' Simon Peter answered him, 'Lord, to whom can we go? You have the words of eternal life. We have come to believe and know that you are the holy one of God.'

Celebrities today come and go, sparkling in the spotlight for a short time before their followers lose interest and move on to the next rising star. The miracle of the feeding led to great crowds following Jesus, but his teaching was too hard and they began to disappear.

There is a poignancy in Jesus' question here, even as it is challenging. Jesus is vulnerable, for even his disciples might turn away. There is a deeper meaning than the words on the surface suggest, for 'going away' implied more than a physical departure. Jesus went on to refer to the betrayal by Judas (vv. 70–71) and although Judas did not leave at this point, he may already have grown cold inwardly and begun his journey towards apostasy. If so, he represents the opposite of Simon Peter's response to Jesus' question, though this too is more complicated than the surface enthusiasm implies. We know how Peter would go on to betray Jesus and go away in every sense from his Lord.

At this point, however, his words challenge us on the deepest level. Where else would we find all that is offered in Jesus? Who else invites us to share life that is eternal? Peter's words are 'believe and know', two favourite words of the writer that encompass what it means to have faith in the one who has revealed the Father's heart. We too have 'come to believe and know', but there is always so much more. As we walk with God each day, the invitation to grow in understanding and deepen our relationship with Jesus is ever present. The eternal life that Jesus offers is one of quality and depth, and each day provides the opportunity to fathom its depth more fully.

Help me to see you more clearly and love you more deeply today, Lord. Amen.

LIZ HOARE

Such learning!

About the middle of the festival Jesus went up into the temple and began to teach. The Jews were astonished at it, saying, 'How does this man have such learning, when he has never been taught?' Then Jesus answered them, 'My teaching is not mine but his who sent me. Anyone who resolves to do the will of God will know whether the teaching is from God or whether I am speaking on my own.'

It is the kind of question we still ask: which school did he go to? What gives her the authority to speak on such and such a topic? John's core question of who Jesus is comes to the fore again in this section. Make no mistake: it really does matter whose teaching we live our lives by.

It was the Jewish Feast of Tabernacles or Booths, recalling the wanderings of God's people in the wilderness under the leadership of Moses. It was a feast characterised by joy and celebration. Thousands of people would have gathered in Jerusalem, and expectations around the promised Messiah would have been heightened. It was in this atmosphere that Jesus went to the temple, the very heart of the Jewish faith, to teach, and once again his identity is under scrutiny. Where did he get his teaching from?

The author is building up the atmosphere of threat as the climax of the narrative draws closer. There is also an edge to the way Jesus says that a person may come to know the truth. In answering the scepticism of his listeners here, Jesus claims that the source of his teaching is God and the way to test this out is through obedience.

Most of us start the other way round, weighing something up before testing it out. But Jesus insists obedience is the way to recognise the truth of his claims, rather than analysing it first. Try it and you will see. Perhaps it is a question of our heart's desire. Are we still clinging to our own will or genuinely wanting to follow in God's way?

'I delight to do your will, O my God; your law is within my heart'
(Psalm 40:8).

LIZ HOARE

An eternally significant cry

On the last day of the festival, the great day, while Jesus was standing there, he cried out, 'Let anyone who is thirsty come to me, and let anyone who believes in me drink. As the scripture has said, "Out of the believer's heart shall flow rivers of living water."' Now he said this about the Spirit, which believers in him were to receive.

It was the final climactic day of the Feast of Booths, and a great deal of controversy had occurred from the time Jesus arrived in Jerusalem to this point. People had argued about him; some had believed, while others tried to have him arrested (vv. 30–31). There was considerable confusion (vv. 35–36). On this final day Jesus made another startling statement about himself, echoing earlier themes already mentioned in John, such as water and Spirit and believing in him. This time, Jesus' statement was also looking ahead to the outpouring of the Spirit after the resurrection.

It is such an important announcement that Jesus cried out as he proclaimed it. Imagine someone standing in a public place today. What would they cry? Something about the latest scientific discovery, or maybe the news that a celebrity was coming to town? Jesus' cry was of eternal significance, making all our worldly concerns seem temporary and mostly trivial. The imagery of the Spirit flowing like rivers of living water implies a never-ending source of life and refreshment for those who come to Jesus and believe. 'Living' water suggests a fresh, free-flowing and endless supply from a source that is pure, reliable and thirst-quenching.

John wants his readers to imagine all this and more. This water flows out of the source of all life itself – the living Word. Jesus claimed to be speaking in harmony with the scriptures, in particular Isaiah 55 and Ezekiel 47, but interpreting them through his mission. Thus instead of water flowing from the temple, as in Ezekiel, in future it would flow out of the individual lives of his followers through the indwelling of the Holy Spirit.

Lord, fill me with your Spirit today and overflow in me
to be a blessing for the world. Amen.

LIZ HOARE

1 Samuel 1—12

Over the next two weeks we will be reading and reflecting on brief extracts from the first twelve chapters of Samuel. This has had to be a selective process, but I hope the people and stories we will focus on will help us trace the meaning and significance of the bigger story.

The books of 1 and 2 Samuel tell of a people journeying from a loose, fiercely independent, tribal confederacy to the beginning of a monarchy and the struggle to grow into one nation under king and God. Its themes have much in common with our own world. There was a preoccupation with finding leadership in insecure times. There was the task of seeking God's presence and searching for meaning in the unsettling events that were shaping their destiny. And that ancient narrative presented challenges to prevailing assumptions about the partnership of women and men and their life together (though this is easily missed).

What makes the storytelling in Samuel so significant is not so much the stories told as *the way it tells them*; not just 'what the Bible says' but *how* it says it.

This ancient saga has grown with the telling, which is how it ended up needing two volumes. The final version of this long narrative was completed nearly 400 years after the nation had been conquered, Jerusalem and the temple destroyed and God's people deported *en masse* to Babylon. There, in a far country, their own land captured, their faith, holy city and temple in ruins, they were sifting through the highs and catastrophic lows of their nation's story and seeking to find God, meaning and wisdom in it all.

The books of Samuel are not to be read like modern histories. Though the narrative follows a broad chronology, there are times when stories and events appear out of sequence or without an obvious reason. Details we might think important are not included, while attention is given to things that to us seem peripheral. It all requires careful attention. In one sense it is more like an experience of open theatre, where we, the audience, form part of the play and are expected to respond to it as it unfolds. This is wisdom literature: recorded for us to listen, learn and apply to our own world.

DAVID RUNCORN

A certain man

There was a certain man of Ramathaim, a Zuphite from the hill country of Ephraim, whose name was Elkanah son of Jeroham son of Elihu son of Tohu son of Zuph, an Ephraimite. He had two wives; the name of one was Hannah, and the name of the other Peninnah. Peninnah had children, but Hannah had no children. Now this man used to go up year by year from his town to sacrifice to the Lord of hosts at Shiloh.

'Once upon a time…' All stories must start somewhere, and all writers choose how they begin. Some stories open dramatically. This one is simply factual. 'A certain man' is formally introduced by his region, tribe, name and family line. His two wives follow him. Publicly, at least, this is a man's world. The women are introduced only by name and their child-bearing status.

'Hannah had no children.' That is a simple statement of fact that conceals great pain and longing, even more so in a culture where a woman's whole worth and status was defined by motherhood. Elkanah has not divorced her, but it is likely he took a second wife because Hannah had not conceived. We will soon learn that theirs is not a happy home.

The setting of the story is now introduced. Elkanah is a devout man. It is his practice to take his family on an annual retreat to worship at the shrine of Shiloh – then the holiest centre of his people's faith. (This story is set before Jerusalem and the temple were in existence.) Bringing his family to Shiloh is, in fact, Elkanah's only significant role in the story that is now beginning. After the first chapter, he is mentioned no more. But he brings his family to the place from whence a brave new era in the history of God's people will begin.

Elkanah comes across as a caring but ineffectual figure. His few recorded words are questions – 'Why?' He simply cannot understand what is going on around him. If something new is to emerge from this faithful but unhappy annual pilgrimage, it will need the unexpected faith and initiative of someone else. And that is exactly what happens.

Pray for understanding in those times when you do not understand what is happening.

DAVID RUNCORN

Hannah

After they had eaten and drunk at Shiloh, Hannah rose and presented herself before the Lord. Now Eli the priest was sitting on the seat beside the doorpost of the temple of the Lord. She was deeply distressed and prayed to the Lord and wept bitterly. She made this vow: 'O Lord of hosts, if only you will look on the misery of your servant and remember me and not forget your servant but will give to your servant a male child, then I will set him before you as a nazirite until the day of his death.'

Hannah is anguished over her continued inability to bear children, mocked by the fertile but insecure Peninnah, and she finds herself once more expected to worship at the shrine of the Lord who has 'closed her womb' (v. 5) – a statement offered factually, without explanation or implying judgement. She now steps centre stage. Entering the shrine, she presents herself before the Lord and pours out her grief-filled prayer.

She has come to God, for he is both her adversary and her ally. He has closed her womb. Only he can choose to open it. While it is true that desperate people will promise *anything*, and Hannah's prayer could sound like bargaining, all that follows suggests that she is making a remarkable offering, born out of costly and profound faith.

Hannah and Eli the priest are sharply contrasted in this scene. Hannah is standing before God in the middle of the temple; Eli is sitting over by the doorway of the temple. Hannah is praying to the Lord; Eli is watching someone else praying. In fact, he cannot even recognise her tearful anguish as prayer at all. He assumes she is drunk. Hebrew storytellers have a number of ways of giving clues and hints to get us to notice important things. One is to emphasise the posture of a lead character. When people are found sitting down, things do not usually go well for them. The faith this story needs is active and alert. Hannah is the model for this.

Her prayer is answered. Yet found here at the beginning, her story is much more than a touching, domestic vignette about where the important figure comes from who will stand astride this great era of Israel's history. Her faith is the key to interpreting all that follows.

Pray for courage and faith like Hannah's though pain and perplexity.

DAVID RUNCORN

Hannah's song

Hannah prayed and said, 'My heart exults in the Lord; my strength is exalted in my God. My mouth derides my enemies because I rejoice in your victory. There is no Holy One like the Lord, no one besides you; there is no Rock like our God... The barren has borne seven, but she who has many children is forlorn... The Lord makes poor and makes rich; he brings low; he also exalts.

Hannah's prayer-filled grief in the temple was not in vain. Her prayer was answered. If this was a film set, the cameras would now be drawing back and wide. The vision becomes cosmic and Hannah sings. A story that began in the private grief of a family home is now proclaimed as a sign of a new world order! The opening of Hannah's 'barren' womb is revealed as a prophetic sign of the Lord's ways in all the world. This song, like that of Mary, centuries later, is one of revolution. She sings of a reversal of fortunes, of a God who raises the powerless and shatters the powerful and who gives life and hope where there had only been despair.

Hannah's prominence at the beginning of this epic narrative is subversive of the prevailing social, institutional and theological powers, which are patriarchal. In fact, whatever story is beginning here, it is not one that the established order of things has any way of understanding. Both Elkanah and Eli are found on the outside of the action, struggling to make sense of what is going on and its significance. Time and again, in the stories that will follow, it will be the initiatives and faith of a woman, named or unnamed, on which the action turns, and God's purposes are furthered.

Whatever will unfold in Israel's history in the long chapters that follow, these opening stories about Hannah should warn us that, whatever is needed, it will not be established by powerful, charismatic personalities or by political or military strategies. It starts – and will end – in a quite different place, led through the vulnerable faith of a woman's story, enabled by her initiative, revealed by her prayer and interpreted by her song.

Pray for Hannah's vision and hope in today's world.

DAVID RUNCORN

Vocation corrupted

Now the sons of Eli were scoundrels; they had no regard for the Lord or for the duties of the priests to the people. When anyone offered sacrifice, the priest's servant would come... with a three-pronged fork in his hand, and... all that the fork brought up the priest would take for himself... Thus the sin of the young men was very great in the sight of the Lord, for they treated the offerings of the Lord with contempt.

The narrator of Samuel does not often reveal their own opinion about the events they are relating. This means that some dreadful stories and behaviours are at times reported apparently without judgement or censure. But it is for *our* discernment that they are recorded.

On the failings of Eli's priestly line, however, the narrator is unambiguously condemning. Though English Bibles translate the word differently, the sons of Eli are denounced with the same severe word with which Eli earlier insulted Hannah (1:14). This will not be the last time we will read of abuse and corruption exercised by those entrusted with the leadership and spiritual care of God's people.

The Christian church has in recent years had to confront scandals of abuse within its communities and among its leaders. Perhaps we can appreciate something of the shock, pain and demoralisation of God's ancient people where leadership has lost all moral integrity. One thing this warns us against is making idealistic assumptions about goodness and innocence in our own faith communities. This is a timely reminder for us today as we begin Lent, the season of self-examination. We must never underestimate the depths from which we need redeeming.

One of the qualities of this long historical reflection is its honesty. It tells it warts and all. In the history writing of that day, kings were treated as semi-mythic gods; their legacy was without taint or failure. By contrast the Bible record could be called post-heroic storytelling. We are invited to learn from failings as well as qualities, the evil as well as the good.

Back in Israel, the narrator is setting the scene for God's saving response to a people that have lost their way. And we trust he will do the same for us.

Pray that I, too, may always live in honesty and truth.

DAVID RUNCORN

Ash Wednesday 57

Remembering

A man of God came to Eli and said to him, 'Thus the Lord has said: I revealed myself to the family of your ancestor in Egypt when they were slaves to the house of Pharaoh. I chose him out of all the tribes of Israel to be my priest, to go up to my altar, to offer incense, to wear an ephod before me, and I gave to the family of your ancestor all my offerings by fire from the Israelites. Why then look with greedy eye at my sacrifices and my offerings and honour your sons more than me by fattening yourselves on the choicest parts of every offering of my people Israel?'

Like a tragic refrain, the narrator keeps returning to catalogue further the grim demise of faith and ministry of the ageing Eli and his family line. But now God gets directly involved. Judgement is spelled out, and it is severe.

It begins as a call to remember where all this began, back with 'your ancestor in Egypt'. Israel's whole existence is traced to their liberation from slavery under Pharaoh. This message is not just for Eli; it is true for all God's people. In the Bible, faith and faithfulness is always rooted in remembrance. And out of that remembrance flows lives of worship and honouring of the God who still calls and saves.

Remembering is much more than having a good memory for dates or events. Remembering is not the opposite of forgetting. It is to be reconnected to things from which we have become separated. Eli and his family are dis-membered from the faith of God's people and their God. They have lost their call that has sustained their family across generations. Their life and ministry is no longer rooted in God's saving work. 'Why?' God asks him.

And alternating with these reports on Eli, the narrator keeps inserting single line updates on the faith and ministry of 'the boy Samuel' (e.g. vv. 18, 21, 26). By complete contrast, he is found without fail in the temple, 'standing before' or 'ministering to' the Lord. Between the lines of a story of lost faith and vocation is something new about to emerge?

Pray for those who have lost faith and the call that is theirs.

DAVID RUNCORN

The call of Samuel

The boy Samuel was ministering to the Lord under Eli. The word of the Lord was rare in those days; visions were not widespread. At that time Eli, whose eyesight had begun to grow dim so that he could not see, was lying down in his room; the lamp of God had not yet gone out, and Samuel was lying down in the temple of the Lord, where the ark of God was.

What is a world like in which God seems to have withdrawn from sight and sound? Does it all go eerily silent? Quite probably it is noisier than ever. When God goes silent, we do not hear nothing, we hear *every*thing. There is nothing to give us focus or perspective, so we are left at the mercy of a chaotic clashing of conflicting, competing messages with no way of discerning priority or meaning in it.

This is the storyteller's diagnosis of those times. Nothing is more serious. Here are a people living out of sight and sound of their God. We might wonder how the storyteller would characterise our own times? In the Bible, the greatest crisis in any age is always about God.

Once again, the two characters in the scene are sharply contrasted. This is vivid storytelling. 'The boy' Samuel is contrasted with the ageing Eli. Samuel is ministering before the Lord; Eli is lying down in a side room. In an age where visions are rare, Israel's priest has almost lost his sight. Their ministering – alive and dying – is contrasted. Yet into this bleak scenario of lost faith and vocation the narrator pencils in a message of vulnerable hope: 'The lamp of God had not yet gone out' (v. 3). The lamp, there in the holy presence of God, symbolises the faith of God's people. It is flickering but not extinguished.

So it is that the silent God is about to speak and kindle new vision. Another storytelling device is to make the first words spoken by a person express something about their character and call. Samuel's first words – repeated four times – are 'Here I am.'

That will sum up his whole long ministry – he will be present, all his life, before God and the people. He will be one through whom people would hear and catch the vision of God.

Here I am, Lord.

DAVID RUNCORN

The ark

In those days the Philistines mustered for war against Israel, and Israel… encamped at Ebenezer… Israel was defeated by the Philistines… The elders of Israel said, 'Why has the Lord put us to rout today before the Philistines? Let us bring the ark of the covenant of the Lord here from Shiloh, so that he may come among us and save us from the power of our enemies.' So the people sent to Shiloh.

The Philistine people embody all that threatens the security and peace of God's people. They have just defeated Israel in war, so the elders of the people meet to discern what has happened. But notice who they say has actually defeated them: God. Their business is with God, but no praying follows. God is not consulted at all. Instead, they send for the ark of the covenant.

In one sense they are right to turn to the ark; it exists to remind them of their history and faith as a people delivered from slavery and captivity by God. But here they are turning it into a kind of magic totem laden with divine powers. Faith is reduced to superstition.

This is a world that believes in magic symbols. In the verses that follow today's passage, the ark strikes terror. But Israel is defeated again, and the ark is captured by the enemy. The chaos continues wherever it goes.

This strange cartoon-like saga of the ark is a warning against attempts to conscript God for our own needs and purposes. Throughout history, armies, leaders and churches have all tried to behave like this. The story exposes such behaviour for the godless, presumptuous folly it always is.

The story ends with the ark resting in quiet isolation on a hilltop. Samuel now reappears and guides the people through repentance. The Philistines are defeated. Order is restored. The place is called 'Ebenezer', meaning 'Thus far the Lord has helped us' (1 Samuel 7:12). The name speaks of remembrance and trusting faith. But Ebenezer is actually where Israel first gathered for war (1 Samuel 4:1). They have come back to the place they started and can now recognise it for the first time. In this remembrance, faith and trust is refocused and the foundation for the future relaid.

Lord, we easily stray. When we do, bring us back to our beginnings.

DAVID RUNCORN

Give us a king (1)

When Samuel became old, he made his sons judges over Israel... Yet his sons did not follow in his ways but turned aside after gain; they took bribes and perverted justice. Then all the elders of Israel gathered together and came to Samuel at Ramah and said to him, 'You are old, and your sons do not follow in your ways; appoint for us, then, a king to govern us, like other nations.'

Samuel is ageing, and the people are becoming anxious about the future, with good reason. A long, settled era of leadership is passing. (To this day Samuel is revered by the three great monotheistic religions of the world – Judaism, Islam and Christianity.) Who will take over from him?

Samuel wanted the leadership to stay in the family, but the unsuitability of his sons is apparent to everyone but himself. This may partly explain why the elders ask not for a successor – another prophet or judge – but instead for something new: a king. Israel had never had a king before. Sometimes an idea appeals simply because it is different. It comes unburdened by the accumulated baggage of history.

Before we focus on the front-stage characters of Samuel, Saul and David, we need reminding that this is a story of the people as a whole. Leadership always happens in the context of history; it does not exist as pure theory that can be plugged into any organisation or business that needs it. It surfaces in response to the desires of an anxious community, of rival power groups, of international and military unrest and of other issues of faith, theology and needs of God's people.

While for some, a monarchy seemed the best way to find security as a nation, for others (as we will see tomorrow), the request for a king was an outright rejection of God's leadership. It usurped the place of Torah (the law of Moses) and undermined the vocation and freedom of God's people by its near irresistible drift towards despotism. Across the scriptures generally, leadership is an idea that sits in tension between the kingship of the Lord, his word and his people's own vocation. And it still does today.

Lord, may we may never forget that our deepest security is in you.

DAVID RUNCORN

Give us a king (2)

But the thing displeased Samuel when they said, 'Give us a king to govern us.' Samuel prayed to the Lord, and the Lord said to Samuel, 'Listen to the voice of the people in all that they say to you, for they have not rejected you, but they have rejected me from being king over them… Now then, listen to their voice; only, you shall solemnly warn them and show them the ways of the king who shall reign over them.'

Blunt it was, and we can be sure the request for a king would not have been made lightly. No one easily tells a man of Samuel's stature and reputation it is time to step aside. Speaking truth to power is never easy.

Samuel was plainly angry and resentful at being rejected. The signs are that he never really got over it. But this judge and prophet was curiously tin-eared in the face of the people's concerns. Why was he even considering appointing his sons to succeed him without acknowledging and confronting their corruption? Eli at least tried to do this with his sons. There is a worryingly self-serving lack of awareness to be found in Samuel at this point. It is not just the people's request that needs challenging; Samuel does too. Samuel goes on complaining at length until God finally points out to him that it is actually he (God) they are rejecting – not Samuel!

The attraction of a king is puzzling for three reasons. First, as noted yesterday, Israel did not 'do' monarchy. This was because God was their king, and this is a tension that never goes away throughout the uneven years of Israel's monarchy. Second, there is an absence of prayer. There is no language of faith or seeking God's guidance anywhere in this story. Third, the request is neither rational nor emotionally intelligent. The people surely knew that the kings of the surrounding nations were routinely cruel, overbearing despots. If one is already suffering under bad leadership, why ask for something even worse? In any case are not God's people, then and now, supposed to be a sign of a *different* way among the nations?

Well, they are warned of all this, but the people are determined. Nevertheless, God, who is gracious, grants their request.

Pray that God make us wiser in our discerning and our choices.

DAVID RUNCORN

Saul the king (1)

There was a man of Benjamin… He had a son whose name was Saul, a handsome young man. There was not a man among the Israelites more handsome than he; he stood head and shoulders above everyone else. Now the donkeys of Kish, Saul's father, had strayed. So Kish said to his son Saul, 'Take one of the young men with you; go and look for the donkeys'… but they did not find them… Saul said to the young man who was with him, 'Let us turn back.'

In obedience to God and at the insistence of the people, Samuel is on the search for Israel's first king. He comes to the prestigious house of Kish and sees the young Saul. Samuel is immediately swayed by his physical appearance (see also 1 Samuel 10:23).

If the emphasis on Saul's good looks and height seems over the top, perhaps it is meant to. The same tendencies are all too familiar in our own world. Did you know that 90% of international business executives are above average height? An extra inch in height is reckoned to be worth an additional $1,000 a year in salary in the international business world. However, now, as then, outward appearances are no guarantee of ability or wisdom, and the story will (belatedly) remind us that God looks on the heart.

Another Hebrew storytelling device is found here. Whenever a person's looks are emphasised, there is usually not a happy outcome. And remember how the first words spoken by a person reveal something of their character? Saul's first words are: 'Let us turn back.' That was one of the fatal flaws of Saul as man and king: he never managed to see anything through. He will spend his life searching for what usually eludes him and struggling to achieve whatever he sets out to do. Little about him is decisive or constant. Very often, as in this opening story, he needs those around him to hold him to his task.

It is therefore not surprising that when the time comes to reveal him as king, Saul goes missing and is found hiding behind some baggage (10:21–23). The stakes are high for king and people, and the warning signs are clear. This may not go well.

Pray for potential leaders being chosen today, wherever they are.

DAVID RUNCORN

Saul the king (2)

Samuel took a vial of oil and poured it on his head and kissed him; he said, 'The Lord has anointed you ruler over his people Israel. You shall reign over the people of the Lord, and you will save them from the hand of their enemies all around... As he turned away to leave Samuel, God gave him another heart... and the spirit of God possessed him.

At the time the monarchy was created, Israel was a loose confederation of tribes, north and south. They were independent and not easy to govern. Getting them to agree together about the choice of a king would have been extremely difficult. The beginning of Saul's kingship reflects this. Saul was first anointed privately by Samuel. It was kept secret. Only later was he publicly revealed to the people, and on that occasion, despite Samuel's best attempts to talk him up, the narrator tells us the public response to Saul was very mixed.

Samuel's presence is also ambiguous in this story. After anointing Saul king, Samuel goes on giving him lengthy instructions. It sounds heavily controlling of someone already lacking in confidence. So what happens next is significant. The briefing meeting over, we are told that as Saul 'turned his back' (literal translation) to leave Samuel, 'God gave him another heart' (v. 9). Symbolically, this is hugely significant. For if Saul is to be a king in his own right, he must turn his back on Samuel and move away from Samuel's controlling presence.

The storyteller knows what must happen if this is going to work. So does God, who now gives his king the heart he needs for the task. Every leader has their own version of this to deal with. We already know that Saul's kingship will ultimately fail. But at this early stage in his reign, both the narrator and God, it seems, believe in the possibility of it. Saul is a man with a tendency to turn back. But at this point, chosen and anointed, he turns towards his own destiny and call, and the Spirit of God fills him.

Pray for those who are struggling to find confidence
for the challenges that face them.

DAVID RUNCORN

Saul and the Ammonites

About a month later, Nahash the Ammonite went up and besieged Jabesh-gilead… All the people wept aloud. Now Saul was coming from the field behind the oxen, and Saul said, 'What is the matter with the people, that they are weeping?' So they told him the message from the inhabitants of Jabesh. And the spirit of God came upon Saul in power when he heard these words, and his anger was greatly kindled.

In those days the Ammonite nation was dominant in the region and was terrorising the surrounding Hebrew tribes on their borders. Their brutality was extreme. The only peace treaty Nahash, their king, would accept was to gouge out one eye from each man from the tribes they conquered. That effectively left them defenceless for years ahead. The Ammonites were now besieging their latest intended victims at Jabesh-gilead. The people were weeping in terror as they anticipated their fate. They had no help to call on. There are places in the world today that know all too well the trauma of such a scenario.

Meanwhile, where is the king? Saul is back at home, ploughing his fields. This horrific story is still set, for all practical purposes, in the familiar old world of tribal allegiances and alliances. King he may be, but it is really only in name at present. He has yet to rule in any sense at all.

As he returns home from the fields, he hears the weeping and catches up with the news. It is, of course, the job of a king to fight wars and defend the people against their enemies. He is suddenly convulsed by the Spirit of God into a raging anger. With a confidence previously unmentioned, a hitherto hesitant man acts with strength, decisiveness and passion. Extreme times need extreme measures. His call to muster is itself a violent threat. But the effect is totally compelling. And lest it be thought that this inexperienced king is simply winging it, the story is careful to detail a military acumen and strategic ability behind his approach to the battle. Under their new king, the people fight and win!

---

*Pray for those who are leading the fight against evil
and protecting the weak today.*

DAVID RUNCORN

Renewing the kingship

Saul said, 'No one shall be put to death this day, for today the Lord has brought deliverance to Israel.' Samuel said to the people, 'Come, let us go to Gilgal and there renew the kingship.' So all the people went to Gilgal, and there they made Saul king before the Lord in Gilgal. There they sacrificed offerings of well-being before the Lord, and there Saul and all the Israelites rejoiced greatly.

Every leader needs an early success, great or small, and every community looks for first signs that their confidence in the person who was appointed was rightly placed. After a stuttering start, leading an uncertain people, King Saul has had resounding military success. This is the best possible news. Defeating enemies and defending the nation are what kings are supposed to do.

Samuel shrewdly seizes the opportunity and gathers all the people at Gilgal, a deeply symbolic place. Here the people of Israel first camped after crossing the Jordan into the land God had promised them. It is a place of beginnings. Here Saul begins his reign for the third time. It is easy to imagine those exuberant and heartfelt celebrations (intermingled with relief). Surely the future was secure?

The response of the people was to make 'offerings of well-being' (v. 15). This offering is unique among the many sacrifices commanded in Leviticus and elsewhere in that there is no petition or request connected to it. It is an offering of joyful gratitude, asking nothing in return. It is a gift to the One who only gives.

Concern for well-being has become significant in business organisations, churches and communities recently, for good reason. There is so much nowadays that is undermining of human health and flourishing. The stress and anxieties of life in an insecure world are apparent everywhere.

This offering reminds us of where our security is found. There is no need to even ask: it is all gift. Julian of Norwich, praying in her own 14th-century times of war and plagues, is famous for her trusting refrain: 'All shall be well, and all shall be well, and all manner of thing shall be well.'

Let us make our offering of joyful gratitude to God.

DAVID RUNCORN

Taking your stand

Samuel said to the people, 'The Lord is witness, who appointed Moses and Aaron and brought your ancestors up out of the land of Egypt. Now, therefore, take your stand so that I may enter into judgement with you before the Lord, and I will declare to you all the righteous acts of the Lord that he performed for you and for your ancestors.'

These opening chapters of the long Samuel narrative close with calls to faith and faithfulness. But there are issues still needing to be resolved. So soon after Saul and the people have celebrated the reaffirmation of the monarchy, we find Samuel is still occupying centre stage. He is announcing his retirement. But his long speech is increasingly aggressive and threatening in tone. By the end of it the people are feeling thoroughly inadequate, insecure and are pleading with him to stay and pray for them. He promises he is not leaving them. His retirement seems to have been indefinitely postponed.

Now it is the people who are addressed directly. In these early stories, 'the people' have often been a faceless, insecure group, lacking initiative and always looking to others to take charge and carry the responsibilities that are actually theirs.

After another reminder of their history and the God who saves, they receive a significant command: 'Now take your stand.' What does this mean? If someone said that to you, what would you think was expected of you?

There is much talk of a crises of leadership in our day. And these are undeniably demanding times to be a leader anywhere in the world. The challenges are very great. What can be more critical is the crisis of 'followship'. If some leaders can, and do, dominate and overpower, it is also true that followers can, and do, undermine and break their leaders. Followers can be unleadable. At its most formative, leadership must work in creative partnership with 'followship'.

'Now take your stand' calls the people of God to faithfully embrace their own call and take their own responsibilities. So do not be too quick to focus on heroic individual personalities in this epic saga. This has been about the emergence of a people. They too must make their stand – and so must we.

Pray that God will teach you to be a responsible follower.

DAVID RUNCORN

Reconciliation

'Reconciliation' is a word often used in church circles, so it is good to be able to explore the term, its biblical roots and its practical application. The theme of reconciliation runs through the Bible, with its resolution in the saving act of Christ on the cross, 'that God was reconciling the world to himself in Christ, not counting people's sins against them' (2 Corinthians 5:19, NIV). Reconciliation is a huge, lifelong task, and the reconciler must be committed to a journey which will not always be pain-free. It begins with an acknowledgement of our brokenness, not only on an individual scale, but in a community and organisational sense as well.

Reconciliation involves careful listening, a willingness to put aside prejudices and preconceived ideas, to engage in dialogue that is not always affirming and rewarding but can be challenging and distressing. Archbishop Desmond Tutu wrote: 'It is not about patting one another on the back and turning a blind eye to the wrong. True reconciliation exposes the awfulness, the abuse, the hurt, the truth.' This will be a painful experience, yet from this can come a new way forward, a deeper understanding, a more profound level of forgiveness.

And it is not all difficulty and pain – the joy of the father when he welcomes his estranged son home in the parable of the prodigal son sets the pattern for celebration and rejoicing as a vital part of the process. Reconciliation is a task for all of us; we are called to be 'Christ's ambassadors' (2 Corinthians 5:20, NIV) as we look for the coming of the kingdom.

I always enjoy writing notes for *New Daylight*, but the writing of these has given me not only enjoyment but also learning and growth. I hope you benefit from reading these notes as much as I did from writing them, and I pray for you the prayer of Pope Francis for the people of Sri Lanka in 2015, torn apart by civil war: 'May all people here find inspiration and strength to build a future of reconciliation, justice and peace for all the children of this beloved land.'

SALLY WELCH

Something is broken

And he said, 'Who told you that you were naked? Have you eaten from the tree from which I commanded you not to eat?' The man said, 'The woman you put here with me – she gave me some fruit from the tree, and I ate it.' Then the Lord God said to the woman, 'What is this you have done?' The woman said, 'The snake deceived me, and I ate.'

For people or situations to need reconciliation, something has to have gone wrong in the first place. Sadly, given our nature as frail and sinful human beings, it inevitably will. The privilege of free choice involves being able to choose wrong as well as right. Our glorious, ever-changing planet comes with natural events that can bring hardship and tribulation, sometimes leading to conflict over scarce resources.

From the beginning, from that first incidence of the exercise of free will to take a wrong action, the seeds of potential conflict have been sown in words and actions. Here, at the start of our story, Adam and Eve have fallen prey to the sweet suggestions of power and influence and, almost without realising it, succumbed to wrongdoing. God confronts them, but even while acknowledging the truth, they seek to evade responsibility by passing the blame onto someone else: 'The woman… gave me some fruit'; 'The snake deceived me.'

Perhaps the first action of reconciliation is to admit there has been wrong – that something is broken and needs to be fixed. There might be a sense of shame or blame – each party involved might feel that they are the victims; perhaps there will be more than one perceived wrongdoer or perpetrator. There might be deep hurt and trauma, real and lasting wounds as well as more trivial grudges and spites.

All these need to be dealt with, but first each of us has to acknowledge our own guilt and error, however slender this is in the face of the wrongs that have been committed against us. Each of us must determine to undertake the work of reconciliation, aware of its challenges and the pain of the process, but committed to its working out to forgiveness and resolution.

Lord Jesus Christ, forgive us and save us. Amen.

SALLY WELCH

Christ the reconciliation

The Son is the image of the invisible God, the firstborn over all creation. For in him all things were created: things in heaven and on earth, visible and invisible, whether thrones or powers or rulers or authorities; all things have been created through him and for him. He is before all things, and in him all things hold together. And he is the head of the body, the church; he is the beginning and the firstborn from among the dead, so that in everything he might have the supremacy. For God was pleased to have all his fullness dwell in him, and through him to reconcile to himself all things, whether things on earth or things in heaven, by making peace through his blood, shed on the cross.

There is a favourite saying in our family, attributed to Archbishop Desmond Tutu (but I suspect it had been in existence since long before it was made famous by him): 'There is only one way to eat an elephant – one bite at a time.' However large the task, however daunting and impossible it might seem, slow and steady determination will see it gradually come under control.

We use the saying in the context of encouraging a teenager to tidy up an unbelievably messy bedroom, or to start a school project that has been left too late. In fact, it applies to any major piece of work or activity which seems overwhelming but somehow must be tackled.

The task of reconciliation can seem like this at the beginning – the wounds are too deep, the damage is too great, the consequences have become embedded in the community or the system. This passage reminds us that nothing is impossible for God, that in sending his Son, 'the firstborn over all creation' (v. 15), down to live among us, to suffer and die for us, the act of reconciliation is not only begun but has been completed through Christ's action on the cross.

Jesus Christ, reconciler, help us to put our hope and trust in you so that we can in confidence take that first 'bite' and begin your holy work of reconciliation. Amen.

SALLY WELCH

Recognition

When the king [Josiah] heard the words of the Book of the Law, he tore his robes. He gave these orders to Hilkiah the priest, Ahikam son of Shaphan, Akbor son of Micaiah, Shaphan the secretary and Asaiah the king's attendant: 'Go and enquire of the Lord for me and for the people and for all Judah about what is written in this book that has been found. Great is the Lord's anger that burns against us because those who have gone before us have not obeyed the words of this book; they have not acted in accordance with all that is written there concerning us.'

Josiah, the young king of Jerusalem, has set his men to work on rebuilding the temple. During the restoration project, the Book of the Law is found by Hilkiah the high priest. Although Deuteronomy commands that this book be read in full to all the people every seven years, this has evidently not been the case. Hilkiah reads it now, and then reads it to Josiah – and the effect is dramatic.

All of us will have had Josiah's experience – that sickening, heart-sinking moment when you realise that something has gone terribly wrong. It might be something as low key as driving slightly too fast past a speed camera or it might be on a much larger and more serious scale. A moment of thoughtlessness or unkindness that leads to the breakdown of a relationship; an error at work with significant consequences; the giving way to a wrong impulse that has far reaching effects – all these can bring about the modern-day equivalent of Josiah tearing his robes in his anguish and remorse, his desire to roll back the clock.

But that moment of recognition is vitally important, because without it, the process of reconciliation cannot begin. We have to realise something has broken before we can work to fix it, and dreadful though that realisation might be, it can contain within it the seeds of a new beginning.

Lord God, help us to examine our lives in the light of your commandments. Give us the wisdom of fresh insight and the courage to make new beginnings. Amen.

SALLY WELCH

Taking action

'You have heard that it was said to the people long ago, "You shall not murder, and anyone who murders will be subject to judgement." But I tell you that anyone who is angry with a brother or sister will be subject to judgement. Again, anyone who says to a brother or sister, "Raca," is answerable to the court. And anyone who says, "You fool!" will be in danger of the fire of hell. Therefore, if you are offering your gift at the altar and there remember that your brother or sister has something against you, leave your gift there in front of the altar. First go and be reconciled to them; then come and offer your gift.'

These challenging words are part of the sermon on the mount. They are from that famous passage where Jesus literally turns our world upside down with his calling for radical discipleship, for a way of life that gives more than it receives, that looks outwards and upwards rather than focusing on our own wishes and desires, that actively works for the coming of the kingdom in every place at every time. Here too Jesus is raising the bar. It is fairly easy not to commit murder, and most of the population manage this quite well. Not getting annoyed with the people you share your life with, and not bearing a grudge for longer than the blink of an eye – well, that is a different matter entirely!

Reconciliation does not happen in isolation, however; it is a community event, and rightly so. For despite the contemporary habits of individualism, personal fulfilment and 'me time', what we do affects a whole community. We can be reconciled to ourselves, but true reconciliation happens between, among and within communities, and it's vitally important work. Jesus urges us on to take action to resolve any issues we have with our community members as a priority. Before even our obligations of worship and praise, of sacrifice and offering, we must work for reconciliation. The time is now, we are told, for later it might be too late.

Lord help me to give reconciliation the priority it deserves in my life. Give me courage to take the first step, energy to seek resolution and love to effect it.

SALLY WELCH

Understanding the stories

God said to Jonah, 'Is it right for you to be angry about the plant?' 'It is,' he said. 'And I'm so angry I wish I were dead.' But the Lord said, 'You have been concerned about this plant, though you did not tend it or make it grow. It sprang up overnight and died overnight. And should I not have concern for the great city of Nineveh, in which there are more than a hundred and twenty thousand people who cannot tell their right hand from their left – and also many animals?'

The story of Jonah is beautiful in its humanity. Jonah has finally accepted God's call to prophesy to the people of Nineveh and has duly done so. They have repented and been saved, and Jonah is furious! Presumably his righteous anger feels thwarted at the presence of so much forgiveness; the sufferings he has undergone have resulted not in retribution but in a new beginning, and Jonah is resentful of this. So God teaches him, through a plant that springs up, provides shade and then dies. Once Jonah has heard his lesson, he understands and appreciates the great compassion of God.

A necessary part of reconciliation is listening to the stories of others. Whether we agree with their interpretation of events, whether their experience is the same as ours, or whether the same happening had a profoundly different effect on them is of secondary importance compared to the vital work of articulating and sharing narratives. A safe space to do so must be created; a place where all feel free to explain and explore, where stories are listened to carefully and thoughtfully and honoured in the telling. This can be profoundly moving – and extremely painful – and should be done with love and sensitivity in an atmosphere of generosity and forgiveness. If so undertaken, however, the effects can be transformative.

Lord God, help me to listen to the stories of others and honour them, even when they disagree with my own understanding of what happened. Give me patience and tolerance, loving kindness and a desire for truth, so that your healing work can be accomplished within all of us. Amen.

SALLY WELCH

Finding common ground

For he himself is our peace, who has made the two groups one... He came and preached peace to you who were far away and peace to those who were near. For through him we both have access to the Father by one Spirit. Consequently, you are no longer foreigners and strangers, but fellow citizens with God's people and also members of his household, built on the foundation of the apostles and prophets, with Christ Jesus himself as the chief cornerstone.

The subject of Paul's letter here is the division between Jews and Gentiles, and the challenges both groups of people were facing as they sought ways of drawing together as 'fellow citizens'. It is important to understand that this division was not merely one of attending a different church, but of two almost completely separate social groups. In verse 12, Paul writes of the Gentiles as being not only 'separate from Christ' but also 'excluded from citizenship in Israel'. But now, Jew and Gentile are united as members of God's household and must learn new ways of living and worshipping together. While each retains their individual humanity, they must work to find common ground – space in which gifts can be used, talents offered for the general good and community built on the cornerstone of Christ.

The work of reconciliation might begin on neutral ground – a place where none of the parties involved have ownership, where all can be welcome on an equal footing. To progress, however, this neutral ground must become *common* ground, as the things which unify are celebrated and those that divide are acknowledged but not given energy. Barriers of ignorance, self-ishness, suspicion, envy and hate must be dismantled in a spirit of loving determination and a longing for healing. Slights and grudges must be over-looked in favour of drawing together as one people, united in love, by love.

Dear Lord and Father of mankind
Forgive our foolish ways!
Reclothe us in our rightful mind,
In purer lives thy service find,
In deeper reverence, praise.
(John Greenleaf Whittier, 1807–92)

SALLY WELCH

Moving into new territory together

'No, please!' said Jacob. 'If I have found favour in your eyes, accept this gift from me. For to see your face is like seeing the face of God, now that you have received me favourably. Please accept the present that was brought to you, for God has been gracious to me and I have all I need.' And because Jacob insisted, Esau accepted it. Then Esau said, 'Let us be on our way; I'll accompany you.'

Jacob has had such an incident-filled life since fleeing from the wrath of Esau, who was deprived of his father's blessing by Jacob's cunning. Having settled for many years in the land of his father-in-law, Laban, relationships have become difficult and he has resolved to return home. The journey itself is not without adventure, and all the time at the back of Jacob's mind is the fear of how Esau will greet him on his return.

He sends gifts to placate Esau, but that does not ease his mind; instead he finds comfort in the promises of God for his future: 'But you have said, "I will surely make you prosper and will make your descendants like the sand of the sea, which cannot be counted"' (Genesis 32:12). Finally they meet, and Jacob is delighted and surprised at Esau's gracious reaction: 'But Esau ran to meet Jacob and embraced him; he threw his arms around his neck and kissed him. And they wept' (Genesis 33:4). The two brothers, reconciled at last, journey on together.

'I'll accompany you' (v. 12) – what glorious, generous, loving words! Once the seeds of reconciliation have been sown, the task of nurturing under-standing, encouraging cooperation and celebrating community begins in earnest. Groups which previously faced each other with hostility can now begin to journey onwards together, caring for each other and sharing each other's burdens as they forge a new path into the future.

Pilgrims, may we travel with you
To that bright, that better land?
Come and welcome, come and welcome,
Welcome to our pilgrim band.
(Fanny Crosby 1820–1915)

SALLY WELCH

Taking action

But Zacchaeus stood up and said to the Lord, 'Look, Lord! Here and now I give half of my possessions to the poor, and if I have cheated anybody out of anything, I will pay back four times the amount.' Jesus said to him, 'Today salvation has come to this house, because this man, too, is a son of Abraham. For the Son of Man came to seek and to save the lost.'

Church communities are great talking shops. Perhaps this is the case with all large institutions, where instigating change of any kind takes a huge amount of effort. The more people are involved with a plan or a decision, the more consultation should take place, so that individuals within a community feel their opinions have been taken into consideration and that they matter to the organisation.

The larger the community, the more claims there are on its resources. Many individuals and groups might have interesting and exciting plans, all of which require input in terms of money, people and time. Such claims must be scrutinised, debated, then ranked in order of priority, so that the allocation of always scarce resources can be made fairly, economically and effectively. So it is not surprising that many a good idea has fallen into a sad heap on the church council floor, suffering from lack of support, energy or enthusiasm.

Reconciliation, however, is not just a 'good idea'; it is an essential part of kingdom work, and it should not be allowed to lie neglected in a corner of the community consciousness, with everyone aware that 'something should be done' about a particular situation, yet with nothing actually happening.

Zacchaeus can be our role model here: no sooner has he been shown the kingdom of God in the form of Christ's generous offering of inclusion, forgiveness, community and new life, than he takes action. For Zacchaeus must offer reparation: he must actively repair the damage he has caused to people and livelihoods by his dishonest dealings. Only then can he be truly reconciled to his community. Jesus replies with corresponding immediacy – 'Today salvation has come to this house' (v. 9).

Lord Jesus, help us respond to your calls to action with energy and love. Today, this very moment. Amen.

SALLY WELCH

Forming new relationships

Near the cross of Jesus stood his mother, his mother's sister, Mary the wife of Clopas, and Mary Magdalene. When Jesus saw his mother there, and the disciple whom he loved standing near by, he said to her, 'Woman, here is your son,' and to the disciple, 'Here is your mother.' From that time on, this disciple took her into his home. Later, knowing that everything had now been finished, and so that Scripture would be fulfilled, Jesus said, 'I am thirsty.' A jar of wine vinegar was there, so they soaked a sponge in it, put the sponge on a stalk of the hyssop plant, and lifted it to Jesus' lips. When he had received the drink, Jesus said, 'It is finished.'

Jesus' saving work on earth is nearly complete. One last task remains: to care for those he is leaving behind. It is presumed that by now Joseph had died, and that other members of Jesus' family are too far away or unable to take on the care of their widowed mother. Clearly the responsibility of caring for Mary has fallen to Jesus, and it is a responsibility he must hand over.

He does not choose a relative, which would be the norm for those times, the net of relationship spreading ever wider as cousins, uncles, nephews are called upon to care for women left alone after the death of a spouse. Rather he chooses 'the disciple whom he loved' for this precious burden; it is John who will take the mother of the Messiah into his home. Only then can Jesus say, with triumph, satisfaction, exhaustion, even relief: 'It is finished' (v. 30).

The work of reconciliation involves forming new relationships, taking the first steps of hospitality and welcome with strangers, hoping that in time they will become friends and companions, forging new links of mutual responsibility and trust, and forming new spirals of blessing as the love that comes from God is shared and returned in praise. It is exciting, challenging work, but as we step out into the unknown, we do so in the company of Christ, our eternal companion and guide.

Lord Jesus, as you walked alongside the disciples on the road to Emmaus, help us to trust that we will never walk alone. Amen.

SALLY WELCH

Reconciliation and celebration

'The elder brother became angry and refused to go in. So his father went out and pleaded with him. But he answered his father, "Look! All these years I've been slaving for you and never disobeyed your orders. Yet you never gave me even a young goat so I could celebrate with my friends. But when this son of yours who has squandered your property with prostitutes comes home, you kill the fattened calf for him!" "My son," the father said, "you are always with me, and everything I have is yours. But we had to celebrate and be glad, because this brother of yours was dead and is alive again; he was lost and is found."'

Thus far it might seem that reconciliation is very hard work, and it can be! Reconciliation demands determination, generosity of spirit, hospitality, energy, engagement, love and hope. But it can bring peace, healing, flourishing communities, personal fulfilment and a renewal of love and hope. So it is only right that reconciliation is partnered with opportunities for celebration and rejoicing – and this passage gives us the perfect justification for that.

The younger son could have been greeted with sternness and possibly even further punishment. But instead there is a spirit of forgiveness and a recognition of new beginnings, of looking to the future. Kindly and gently, the father explains this to the elder son, the one who has not needed reconciliation because he worked hard at the relationship, did his duty and satisfied his obligations. Once forgiveness has been sought and received, once lessons have been learnt and new starts made, then we must look forwards, not backwards. As Jesus tells us: 'No one who puts a hand to the plough and looks back is fit for service in the kingdom of God' (Luke 9:62).

So let us honour those who were far off and who have drawn near. Let us celebrate with those whose relationships were broken but are now being mended. Let us rejoice with those who have been healed, gathering in praise to the one who is the source of all life.

'Praise the Lord… Praise him for his acts of power; praise him for his surpassing greatness… Let everything that has breath praise the Lord'
(Psalm 150:1–2, 6).

SALLY WELCH

A lifelong process

So Boaz took Ruth and she became his wife. When he made love to her, the Lord enabled her to conceive, and she gave birth to a son. The women said to Naomi: 'Praise be to the Lord, who this day has not left you without a guardian-redeemer. May he become famous throughout Israel! He will renew your life and sustain you in your old age. For your daughter-in-law, who loves you and who is better to you than seven sons, has given him birth.' Then Naomi took the child in her arms and cared for him. The women living there said, 'Naomi has a son!' And they named him Obed. He was the father of Jesse, the father of David.

Ruth and Naomi came from different lands. Naomi and her family were driven into the land of Moab by famine. Her two sons took Moabite women as wives, but tragedy struck and the males all died. The two women set aside the differences of race and land in the face of hardship. Together they survived widowhood, a long journey and the perils of living on the poverty line and being forced to gather crops from the edges of fields to avoid starvation.

With Naomi's help, Ruth has negotiated a respectable marriage with a righteous kinsman, thus stabilising the future for both women. Now, Ruth has given birth to a son, securing the male line – a just reward for her faithfulness in following her mother-in-law back to her homeland. Obed is more than just a sign of reconciliation, he is a promise of the future, as the line he begins will end with the Messiah, the redeemer of the world.

Reconciliation is a lifelong process. It may last beyond a lifetime, in fact, as each succeeding generation learns to recognise, to listen, to set aside its differences, to offer and receive forgiveness, and to commit to peace. It is a journey that cannot be accomplished without God, as it is only through Christ's reconciling action that we will meet our final destination.

Lord God, help me not to 'forgive and forget', but to 'forgive and go forward'
in love and peace. Amen.

SALLY WELCH

The ministry of reconciliation

All this is from God, who reconciled us to himself through Christ and gave us the ministry of reconciliation: that God was reconciling the world to himself in Christ, not counting people's sins against them. And he has committed to us the message of reconciliation. We are therefore Christ's ambassadors, as though God were making his appeal through us. We implore you on Christ's behalf: be reconciled to God. God made him who had no sin to be sin for us, so that in him we might become the righteousness of God.

I distinctly remember the first time I was licensed as a parish priest. The bishop of Reading, at that time Rt Revd Dominic Walker, took the service and solemnly pronounced the words: 'Receive this cure of souls which is both yours and mine.' The 'cure', or care, of every member of the parish was my responsibility – shared with the bishop, but in day-to-day matters, mine alone. The bishop of Oxford in his blog describes this 'cure': 'At its centre is the ministry of reconciliation between individuals and God and between people and communities through the death and resurrection of Jesus Christ' (**blogs.oxford.anglican.org/the-cure-of-souls**).

But it is not meant to be held by priests alone, as this passage makes clear. To every single one of us is given the ministry of reconciliation. Every single Christian is one of Christ's ambassadors, pleading for the work of repentance, forgiveness, peace and reconciliation to be carried out in every generation, in every community.

This is a serious task and one which cannot be effected simply by laws or licences. As Nelson Mandela writes: 'In the end reconciliation is a spiritual process which requires more than just a legal framework. It has to happen in the hearts and minds of people.' This is where we come in, using our words and actions, our speech and gestures, our attitudes and approaches to advocate for reconciliation, for the mending of the brokenness of humanity, made possible by the breaking of bread.

Lord God, Father of humanity, help me to not only speak about reconciliation but act on it too.

SALLY WELCH

Building structures that reflect values

They devoted themselves to the apostles' teaching and to fellowship, to the breaking of bread and to prayer... All the believers were together and had everything in common. They sold property and possessions to give to anyone who had need. Every day they continued to meet together in the temple courts. They broke bread in their homes and ate together with glad and sincere hearts, praising God and enjoying the favour of all the people. And the Lord added to their number daily those who were being saved.

I have a weakness for 'lifestyle shops' – those places where everything you 'need' is on offer, from scented candles to luxury bath products, faux fur throws and huge potted palms. I can wander round for hours, imagining a life where these are part of my everyday, where everything is easy and relaxed and there is no such thing as elderly relatives, tricky pastoral issues or an oven that needs cleaning.

I am aware of the shallowness of this way of thinking, and it is one I indulge in only when I am in need of time away from the realities of life. For no amount of curated bookshelves or handcrafted jars of pickle will compensate for a life that is lived according to God's purposes, one that is generous and loving, where the gifts and talents we have been given are used for the benefit of others, and peace and justice are goals which are actively and constantly sought.

Reconciliation is a 'lifestyle choice'. Just as those first Christians lived in community, sharing all that they had and praising God, so we as reconcilers must commit to a lifetime of careful listening, of patient forgiveness, of steady progress towards mutual understanding of the needs of others. The life of those first disciples was lived in harmony with each other, with a generosity of spirit that enabled everything to be held in common. This goal is not easily won, but it is worth the effort.

'Our ultimate end must be the creation of the beloved community'
(Martin Luther King, Jr, 1929–68).

SALLY WELCH

The promise

Then I saw 'a new heaven and a new earth,' for the first heaven and the first earth had passed away, and there was no longer any sea... And I heard a loud voice from the throne saying, 'Look! God's dwelling-place is now among the people, and he will dwell with them. They will be his people, and God himself will be with them and be their God. "He will wipe every tear from their eyes. There will be no more death" or mourning or crying or pain, for the old order of things has passed away.'

Sadly, reconciliation isn't always possible in this world. Sometimes the wounds are too deep to heal, pouring out lifeblood on a daily basis until the injured are mere shadows, condemned to live a half-life of pain and trauma. Sometimes an event so twists and bends a character and personality that the rest of the days on earth are viewed through a distorting lens of bitterness and hatred. Sometimes the seed of evil has sunk so deep into a soul that it has taken root, choking out goodness and love like a weed, spreading and strangling throughout.

We do not lose hope, however, but put our trust in the coming of the kingdom, the final reconciliation, when earth and heaven are renewed, when all is healed. We celebrate our faith in God's loving purposes for all humanity, even though at the moment we might only see 'through a glass, darkly' (1 Corinthians 13:12, KJV). We rejoice in the second chances we get, which don't actually stop at two but continue in an outpouring of grace upon us. And we put our trust in the goodness of one whose love for us was so great that he sent his Son to live among us and to die for us and for our sins, so that we might escape the final punishment of death.

This is God, whose last whisper to us, in the midst of all the darkness, is a promise: 'I am the resurrection and the life. The one who believes in me will live, even though they die' (John 11:25).

'Where, O death, is your victory? Where, O death, is your sting?'
(1 Corinthians 15:55).
'Lord, make me an instrument of your peace'
(Francis of Assisi, c. 1181–1226).

SALLY WELCH

1 Timothy

Today there are so many different ways in which we can communicate with each other: telephone, email, social media, to name but a few. So when a handwritten letter tumbles on to the front door mat, it feels not only strange but somehow also magical and special. Someone has taken the time and trouble to physically put pen to paper and write to you.

Paul was an avid letter writer, sending papyrus missives to many of the churches he had founded across Asia Minor and in some cases to individuals. Though much of the content would have been read by the community, when Paul first wrote to Timothy it was to address him directly, guiding, urging and reassuring him as he sought to lead the Christian church at Ephesus. Hence 1 Timothy, along with 2 Timothy and Titus, are often referred to as the 'pastoral letters' as they seek to give advice on the pastoral issues these church leaders were facing.

The early church was in no doubt that this letter was written by Paul and dated it to around the end of Paul's life. But modern scholars have questioned this assumption, arguing that the language and content differs from Paul's other letters as well as pointing to the fact that it counters heresies of the second century. This difference could be explained if someone was writing on behalf of Paul. We know that Paul often used a secretary, and if this person were given some freedom in writing it could explain the difference in language and tone.

Its form is also reminiscent of Paul's other letters. Opening with standard words of salutation and a personal greeting to Timothy, it goes on to outline the main issue of false teaching before giving advice on how to build up the church community, ending with an individual note to Timothy. While the letter raises a number of puzzling questions there is nothing that categorically shows it could not be written by Paul.

So as we pick this ancient letter up from our doormats to ponder over in the next week, let us be aware that we are reading someone else's post. A letter which has been sent on to us from a past time because it holds so much we can still live by and learn from even today.

EMMA PENNINGTON

Who is Timothy?

Paul, an apostle of Christ Jesus by the command of God our Saviour and of Christ Jesus our hope, To Timothy, my true child in the faith: Grace, mercy and peace from God the Father and Christ Jesus our Lord.

Who was Timothy and how did he know Paul? The answers to these questions are pieced together from the many references to him dotted across the letters of Paul and the book of Acts. By gathering the bits and pieces together, a picture emerges of a young man whose mother was Jewish and father Greek. His home was Lystra near Konya in modern-day Turkey, and he probably converted to Christianity when Paul and Barnabas passed through that way on their first missionary journey.

When Paul returned a few years later with Silas, Timothy had become so well-respected for his faith and devotion that Paul decided to take Timothy with him. From then on Timothy became a loyal, trusted and greatly beloved companion, travelling with Paul to his many churches and acting as an envoy on his behalf. In his letters, Paul often refers to Timothy as his 'son in the faith'. The numerous references paint a picture of a young man who was not naturally brave and often unwell, but with Paul's frequent words of reassurance he grew in confidence.

At the time Paul wrote his first letter to him, Timothy was in Ephesus, supervising the local Christian communities and especially being responsible for choosing and training the church leaders. This was not an easy or insignificant position for Timothy and reveals the faith Paul had in him. Ephesus itself was a significant and wealthy city, lying on the axis of a number of trade routes. It was home to the great temple of Artemis as well as Hellenistic mystery religions and many Jews, all of which exerted their influence on the religious climate in the city. Into this heady atmosphere Paul sends a letter that is full of personal reassurance and encouraging words to his beloved son Timothy to help him in his hard task of directing the church on how it should function, behave and act.

We give thanks for all those who have encouraged us in our faith and pray that we may do the same for others.

EMMA PENNINGTON

Staying on the path

I urge you, as I did when I was on my way to Macedonia, to remain in Ephesus so that you may instruct certain people not to teach different teachings and not to occupy themselves with myths and endless genealogies that promote speculations rather than the divine training that is known by faith. But the aim of such instruction is love that comes from a pure heart, a good conscience and sincere faith.

One of the games I loved to play as a child was walking along the edge of the kerb of the pavement to see how far I could get without falling off. I found I could walk along it rather easily, so easily that I soon forgot to look down or concentrate and it was then that my balance went and I found myself in the gutter. In the book of Revelation it is exactly this which the Lord has against the church in Ephesus – that they have 'abandoned the love you had at first' (Revelation 2:4). In other words they have no longer kept their focus on Christ but have fallen into a strange world of superstition and speculation.

In Paul's time, Ephesus was one of the largest and most important of the Roman cities in the western province of Asia. It was at the crossroads of trade and pilgrimage with people from many different backgrounds meeting to trade and worship at the great temple of Artemis. When Paul first arrived in Ephesus, there was a tremendous response to his preaching, as well as hostility. Many Christian groups sprung up and Paul was quickly aware how vulnerable they would be to dubious teaching (Acts 20:29–30).

Ten years on and Paul's fears had materialised, with apocryphal Jewish legends and strange family trees becoming the basis of peculiar teaching. As a former Pharisee, Paul knew this was a misuse of the Jewish law and Christian heritage which needed to be corrected. Timothy is urged and commissioned to bring the churches back to the faith and end this false teaching, which leads them to slip off the kerb.

Lord, help us to keep our eyes focused on Christ and catch us when we fall, so that we may walk this path of life with faith, love and a clear conscience. Amen.

EMMA PENNINGTON

Recipe for reality

I desire, then, that in every place the men should pray, lifting up holy hands without anger or argument, also that the women should dress themselves in moderate clothing with reverence and self-control, not with their hair braided or with gold, pearls, or expensive clothes, but with good works, as is proper for women who profess reverence for God.

I have a theory that there are three kinds of cooks in the world. First, there are those who, preparing a meal, open a recipe book, methodically weigh out the ingredients and follow the instructions to the letter. Then there are those who look up a recipe and, with artistic flair, guess at measurements with the flick of the wrist and a 'that's about right' abandon. Finally, there are those who do not get out the recipe book at all and every meal is a creation of culinary delight or utter disaster.

Paul is decidedly the first kind of cook. Perhaps it is his upbringing as a Pharisee 'devout to the law', but he likes to follow the recipe to create the church of Christ. To an extent this is exactly what was needed in the heady world of Ephesus where anything goes in terms of devotion to Artemis. For the fragile Christians of Ephesus, and Timothy, it must have come as a relief to be given such a clear template for how men and women are to behave and their place in the life of the church community.

But for many today, reading this second chapter leaves a bad taste in the mouth or an upset stomach. The recipe may not suit our modern palate anymore, but Paul's desire to root our lives in prayer and following Christ is as real today as ever it was in the first century. I wonder whether Christ is calling us to leave the cookery book on the shelf and instead trust in his creative culinary skills, which always present a banquet of heavenly delights before us, where all are fed and included.

O Christ, give us grace to follow you alone and so to discern your will and word in our complex lives and to treat others with compassion and kindness.

EMMA PENNINGTON

Feet on the ground, head in the clouds

I hope to come to you soon, but I am writing these instructions to you so that, if I am delayed, you may know how one ought to behave in the household of God, which is the church of the living God, the pillar and support of the truth. Without any doubt, the mystery of godliness is great: He was revealed in flesh, vindicated in spirit, seen by angels, proclaimed among gentiles, believed in throughout the world, taken up in glory.

It's staggering just what you can search for on the internet today. For example, did you know that the old adage 'feet on the ground, head in the clouds' is found in 7,790 lyrics, used by 109 artists and occurs in 50 albums? It also perfectly sums up Paul's third chapter of his letter to Timothy. Trying to set firm foundations for the church, Paul sets out in practical terms just who should be chosen as bishops and deacons. Paul has his feet firmly fixed on the ground as he describes how church leaders need to root the faith of Christ within the living, earthly reality of the Christian community. But at the same time to still to have their heads in the heavens.

As Paul comes to the end of this chapter, he has slipped into this realm of the heavens as his words turn into a song which articulates the mystery of faith. Paul probably did not compose the doxology that closes this chapter; it was likely rather a hymn of praise already known to him and possibly the Ephesians. If you want to know who Christ is, then here you have it: God is revealed in flesh through the incarnation of Jesus, and shown through the work of the Holy Spirit in people's lives. This gospel of reconciliation is announced among Gentiles and believed in throughout the world, and finally Christ takes the path of glory, bringing not only heaven to earth but now earth to heaven in one great leap of faith.

So with his head in the heavens and feet on the ground, Paul encourages his church through Timothy to bring the sparkle of heaven into ordinary life.

How might your reveal this mystery and glorious truth in your own earthly life today.

EMMA PENNINGTON

Searching for truth

For everything created by God is good, and nothing is to be rejected, provided it is received with thanksgiving, for it is sanctified by God's word and by prayer. If you put these instructions before the brothers and sisters, you will be a good servant of Christ Jesus, nourished on the words of faith and of the sound teaching that you have followed. Have nothing to do with profane and foolish tales. Train yourself in godliness.

How do you know if something is true or false? In a world of fake media this has become an even more difficult question to answer. How do you know if the news headlines really depict the truth of a situation or if it is fabricated? The search for truth has become increasingly difficult to navigate. This is not necessarily a modern problem. Timothy was grappling with the same issues in first-century Ephesus, where cults, myths, spurious genealogies and superstition were rife, let alone a muddling of these folk religions with that of the stories of Jesus and the faith in Christ.

In circumstances such as these, where truth is hard to discern from falsehood, it helps to have an outsider, someone who is at a distance and can give some objective advice. Paul stands in this position and can give Timothy that valuable advice and wisdom he needs to navigate between what is true and what is false. Like Ignatius of Loyola, Paul gives Timothy the spiritual tools of discernment to bring not only to ordinary decisions in life, but also to teachings that he may hear around him.

At the heart of this process of discernment is a simple demarcation which is based upon the question of whether something turns us towards or away from God. Whatever is true and holy, whatever is godly, Paul says, then follow this; whatever takes you down a path away from God, this is false. Thus Paul advises Timothy to 'train yourself in godliness' (v. 7) in as rigorous a way as an athlete.

O God, give us grace to cling to Christ that through his truth we may be given the eyes to discern and behold your goodness within all of your creation.

EMMA PENNINGTON

Being 'people' people

Pay close attention to yourself and to your teaching; continue in these things, for in doing this you will save both yourself and your hearers. Do not speak harshly to an older man, but speak to him as to a father, to younger men as brothers, to older women as mothers, to younger women as sisters – with absolute purity.

A bishop was once asked on the day of her retirement, 'What was the best part of your job?' Without hesitation she replied 'People' and then she was asked, 'And what was the worst part?' 'People.' We all have those whom we get on with better than others, but it is to how we treat the 'others' that Paul now turns. For Paul the answer is quite clear, we treat other people as we would our own family. For many today this is not necessarily a helpful analogy, as it can easily isolate and appear hypocritical when the church does not live up to the high ideals of family love, inclusion and loyalty.

But Paul is not necessarily making a value judgement about our personal relationships. He is not basing our relationships with each other on whether we like or get on with the other. Instead he is pointing to a bond that holds diverse people in relationship even when we find we just cannot be in the same room with them. This bond is our faith in Christ, and he sees this as the benchmark that shapes and governs how we treat each other.

There is something deeper and stronger than our personal relationships, however good or bad they may be, that holds us together and governs how we behave to each other. Paul describes it in familial terms – the respect due to a mother, father, sister or brother – duties which were well defined in first-century Asia Minor. For Paul these duties were not limited to blood but formed the bedrock of relationships within the Christian family. We may not associate them as strongly with the image of the family today but the values of respect, loyalty, honour, equity and belonging can still speak as powerfully.

Lord, strengthen within us your values that we might navigate our personal relationships based on faith in Christ rather than our personal preferences.

EMMA PENNINGTON

False teaching

But as for you, man of God, shun all this; pursue righteousness, godliness, faith, love, endurance, gentleness. Fight the good fight of the faith; take hold of the eternal life to which you were called and for which you made the good confession in the presence of many witnesses. In the presence of God, who gives life to all things, and of Christ Jesus… I charge you to keep the commandment without spot or blame until the manifestation of our Lord Jesus Christ.

In the final chapter of this short letter, Paul turns once more to the problem of false teaching. It is the one theme that has run throughout this letter, revealing how perturbed Paul was by it. For Paul, following Christ is not a matter of simply obeying a list of dos and don'ts, following a neatly pre-scribed rule. This must have been both liberating and troubling for Paul. With no more rule book, how do I know I am truly following Christ, and how do I measure whether I am right or wrong in what I think and believe?

Paul realised that, first and foremost, following Christ is about our relation-ship with him, which he discovered on the road to Damascus. Now he reminds Timothy that it is Timothy's relationship with Christ that matters – his love, faith, righteousness, endurance – all that flows from being rooted in Christ with eyes set on him and not the muddling words that he hears around him.

But Paul is also aware that at times this can feel like hard work, a battle even. It is then that he advises Timothy, and us, to 'take hold of eternal life' (v. 12), not as a prize to be won at the end of our lives but as the golden thread of life that links us and holds us to the person of Christ now.

In one of her visions, the 14th-century anchoress Julian of Norwich is approached by the devil in her hour of desperation and despair. As she looks on this hideous image, which sought to terrify and demoralise her, she laughs in its face because she realises the golden truth that Christ has conquered and the devil has no power over her.

Lord, help us in own way to walk in the freedom of that eternal truth which no false teaching can ultimately obscure, that Christ has called us into relationship with him and shapes our lives and relationships with others to reveal heaven on earth now.

EMMA PENNINGTON

Parables of passion

The cross in Matthew's gospel is a world-shaking event whose meanings constantly split and spill through the old conceptual wineskins. Jesus predicted his death, realising that he would share the fate of previous prophets who had announced God's judgement to a 'wicked generation'. Jesus taught his disciples about a new era to which his sacrifice belonged, and he often did this in parables.

Parables are ideal vehicles for exploring the meaning of the cross. They can prod us into reimagining how things should be and help us to discern where God's kingdom is already breaking in. Parables make present future possibilities. In parables, those wise enough to make provision for the bridegroom's arrival can already be rewarded and the consequences of foolishly forgetting can be dramatically anticipated.

Jesus not only spoke in parables, he also acted in parables. What should the crowds make of someone riding into the royal city on a donkey? The fact that Matthew needs to explain that this action fulfils prophecy underlines that its meaning was not obvious. It was certainly far from obvious to the residents of Jerusalem. However, it was the best way for the Messiah to enact the shock of the new.

As Jesus makes his way to the cross, other characters cross his path who also act on him. Their actions either fit with or work against the age to come and are therefore, in a secondary sense, parables of good or evil. The woman brings her ointment to anoint Jesus for burial, while Pilate washes his hands before the crowds to separate himself from justice, and soldiers put a scarlet robe on Jesus and plait a crown of thorns to mock him.

To understand the cross better, we must enter the world of the cross created by these parables. As we do, we shall feel and inhabit more of what it means to live for the coming kingdom. And we shall make the most surprising discovery of all, that the cross can become a burden borne lightly in the hands of love, and that the events leading up to Jesus' death, seemingly signs of weakness and defeat, are in fact the way by which all God's meek ones will come to inherit the earth.

ROLAND RIEM

Beyond fair

Now when the first [worker] came, they thought they would receive more; but each of them also received a denarius. And when they received it, they grumbled against the landowner, saying, 'These last worked only one hour, and you have made them equal to us who have borne the burden of the day and the scorching heat.' But he replied to one of them, 'Friend, I am doing you no wrong; did you not agree with me for a denarius?'

These words, towards the end of the parable of the labourers in the vineyard, set the tone for Jesus' impending passion. There is a massive injustice here to come to terms with. Why should those who have hardly needed to break sweat be paid the same amount as others who have borne the burden of a sweltering full day's toil? This is simply not right nor fair.

No one begrudges generosity. It is up to the landowner if he wants to pay his workers at a higher hourly rate. The issue comes with paying the same to all regardless of their effort. This is what causes the complaint.

But God's action is not tailored to our notions of fairness; it is based on firmer grounds. The first is that everything is the Creator's to give or withhold in the first place, including what we feel we have earned or make claim to own outright. They are his because everything has its being in and through him. The second ground is that this giving or withholding is by God's choice alone. Every choice, whatever it is, springs ultimately from God's unfailing generosity to all.

Both these reasons are echoed in the landowner's response to the worker's complaint: 'I choose to give to this last the same as I give to you. Am I not allowed to do what I choose with what belongs to me?'

Jesus will go to the cross not because it is fair or because some deserve deliverance more than others; he will go out of choice, not his own firstly, but in obedience to the Creator's choice for the world, in whose boundless generosity Jesus delights to dwell, even as others around strive for a far narrower, partial justice.

Is the Lord not allowed to choose how to be generous and just?

ROLAND RIEM

The triumph of meekness

The disciples went and did as Jesus had directed them; they brought the donkey and the colt and put their cloaks on them, and he sat on them. A very large crowd spread their cloaks on the road, and others cut branches from the trees and spread them on the road. The crowds that went ahead of him and that followed were shouting, 'Hosanna to the Son of David! Blessed is the one who comes in the name of the Lord! Hosanna in the highest heaven!'

Jesus not only spoke in parables, he also acted parabolically, in prophetic signs whose extreme strangeness provoked attention and wonder. Our habit of bringing donkeys into church on Palm Sunday may have blunted a sign so shockingly odd: the one who was supposed to bring national deliverance arriving in such an ungainly fashion.

This sign was no accident. Jesus had earlier sent two of his disciples to fetch the donkey and her colt, just so that he could arrive in Jerusalem in this way. Matthew points out that this fulfilled a prophecy that announced to the city's population, the 'daughter of Zion' that their king was coming, 'humble, and mounted on a donkey, and on a colt, the foal of a donkey' (Matthew 21:5).

The people of Jerusalem are thrown into confusion by his manner of arrival. The crowd, however, at this point in the gospel, show their purest faith in Jesus, acclaiming that he has come in the name of the Lord to restore the fortunes of their people. Not until later, under the baleful influence of their leaders, do they forsake his kingship for the favour of an earthly ruler.

Jesus' entry into Jerusalem provokes the crowd to see and believe. In the sermon on the mount he taught, 'Blessed are the meek, for they will inherit the earth' (Matthew 5:5). Now he comes in meekness, in an awkward procession, pulling along a foal, abolishing all pretence of pomp and circumstance. He does not ride these two beasts to fulfil a prophecy; rather, this prophecy fulfils to the letter the sheer meekness of his coming, in and among those who strew his way with palms.

So we pray from the crowd: Jesus our King, may the triumph of your meekness be our way too.

ROLAND RIEM

Faithful tenancy

'Then he sent his son to them, saying, "They will respect my son." But when the tenants saw the son, they said to themselves, "This is the heir; come, let us kill him and get his inheritance." So they seized him, threw him out of the vineyard, and killed him. Now when the owner of the vineyard comes, what will he do to those tenants?' They said to him, 'He will put those wretches to a miserable death and lease the vineyard to other tenants who will give him the produce at the harvest time.'

The way Matthew frames the parable of the wicked tenants makes obvious its immediate target: the law has come, and the prophets too, to remind God's tenant people of their duty to yield to the owner of vineyard Israel his due. Even the owner's son has been sent but treated most cruelly of all. This violent rejection can only bring the severest judgement, because 'the stone that the builders rejected has become the cornerstone' (Matthew 21:42).

Matthew's community, around the time of a painful split with the Jewish synagogue and in the middle of an argument about which tradition was the true heir to God's promises, did not have the headspace to do more with this parable than point it squarely at their rivals. But parables are always capable of generating fresh and provocative meanings for those with ears to hear.

Problems for tenants begin when they start to forget their obligations to the landlord. This is easy to do when you inhabit a property or work on land day by day. The landlord's rightful claims begin to fade, and a false mindset grows. Messages meant to establish healthy relations come to be seen as unwarranted and threatening interventions, and the relationship breaks down.

Dare we read this parable against ourselves, or do we see ourselves as Christian tenants with inalienable rights? As we shall see in tomorrow's reading, though, Matthew believed that places in the kingdom of heaven can be forfeited. For him the proof of our good standing lies in fruitful works stemming from obedience to Jesus, who, as Paul reminds us, even as God's Son 'did not consider equality with God something to be used to his own advantage' (Philippians 2:6, NIV).

Lord, save us from complacency; save us for humility.

ROLAND RIEM

No robe

'But when the king came in to see the guests, he noticed a man there who was not wearing a wedding robe, and he said to him, "Friend, how did you get in here without a wedding robe?" And he was speechless. Then the king said to the attendants, "Bind him hand and foot, and throw him into the outer darkness, where there will be weeping and gnashing of teeth." For many are called, but few are chosen.'

The parable of the wedding banquet is a favourite for those wanting to emphasise the breadth of God's mercy: when the original invitees in the story reject his invitation, the king who is giving a wedding banquet commands his slaves to scour the highways and byways to fill his vast wedding hall. Good and bad together end up at the banquet.

Matthew's version of the story does not end there, however. We get a better look at the guests, and someone has come inappropriately dressed. It is hard not to believe that two originally separate stories have been joined together here, because one can hardly blame someone who may have been whisked from highway to hall for not coming in the right robe.

Nonetheless, there is continuity with the theme of weddings and a strong lesson at the allegorical level, where the twist in the plot hides a deeper and coded truth. This is that God's wide mercy, expressed in the first part of the story, should never, once received, be taken for granted by its recipients.

The guest who is challenged can offer no excuse because, in the second part of the story, everyone is already inside the hall and all those inside should know the proper wedding etiquette. The robe is important for what it might stand for; it might symbolise baptism or good works or maybe both. The point is that any invitee wanting to stay at the party cannot manage without it.

'Many are called, but few are chosen' (v. 14). There is no room for complacency for anyone sitting at the feast – at worship, in prayer, feeding on word and sacrament. The few may be many in the end, there by a triumph of mercy, but no one stays there by default.

Lord, may good works be the full fruit of your mercy towards us. Amen.

ROLAND RIEM

The brooding God

'Jerusalem, Jerusalem, the city that kills the prophets and stones those who are sent to it! How often have I desired to gather your children together as a hen gathers her brood under her wings, and you were not willing! See, your house is left to you, desolate. For I tell you, you will not see me again until you say, "Blessed is the one who comes in the name of the Lord."'

With the strong emphasis on impending judgement in Matthew's gospel, we must be sensitive to the bigger theological picture to prevent our image of God from becoming warped. God is indeed likened to a landowner demanding his dues and to an angry king forcing people to a wedding banquet, but these likenesses are given in parables, stories which both conceal and reveal who God is.

There are other parts of the gospel which are not stories but which, like parables, rely on a transfer of meaning. Here Jesus' lament over Jerusalem contains a beautiful simile from the natural world: his desire to gather up the children of Jerusalem is like a hen gathering her brood under her wings.

Hens are not particularly intelligent animals, but they have fierce protective instincts to ensure the survival of the species. Protecting her chicks is what a hen is for. When Jesus uses the image, therefore, he is saying something fundamental about his mission, to protect his children from the evils and storms of this world.

But Jesus' words reach far beyond instinct. They are filled with pathos as he looks over Jerusalem, the city that will betray his kindness. We see in this heart-rending juxtaposition between the outstretched wings of Jesus and the hostility of his chicks a direct link to the outstretched arms of Jesus on the cross and the taunts and accusations of those around him.

And there is real ardour in this figure of speech. Jesus is not seeking to punish the people of Jerusalem; their punishment lies in spurning his wings. This is where chicks would be safe from perishing and could grow into their full stature. Christ the mother hen grieves their loss and longs for the day all will come to nestle in his warm and welcoming presence.

Under the shadow of your wings, we are safe. Amen.

ROLAND RIEM

Budding hope

'From the fig tree learn its lesson: as soon as its branch becomes tender and puts forth its leaves, you know that summer is near. So also, when you see all these things, you know that he is near, at the very gates. Truly I tell you, this generation will not pass away until all these things have taken place. Heaven and earth will pass away, but my words will not pass away.'

Matthew's gospel is full of apocalyptic imagery, especially as it approaches Jesus' last days. Something cataclysmic is irrupting to shake the foundations of the world order. When our own world appears stable, we may find the prospect difficult to comprehend, but in times of upheaval, especially when the shockwaves touch our own lives, this vision comes to make sense and bring comfort.

The world where holy places are desecrated, where false messiahs and prophets are proclaimed, where the threat of violence and the need to flee is real, is not a distant one. Refugees making their way to our shores across Europe remind us of it daily. The UK itself has not been immune to waves of instability of different kinds and causes, and we see no end to it. Apocalypse, however, says that the end is in sight, that an upending deliverance is indeed on the way.

Jesus' parable of the fig tree has a vital lesson to teach us. It forces us to look carefully at a natural process – the budding of the fig tree. Just before its leaves come out, the branches become tender. If you really look, you will see sure signs of change, and not just any change, but the change from winter straight to summer.

Summertime is the coming of the Son in a blaze of glory, sending out his angels to 'gather his elect from the four winds' (Matthew 24:31). It will be sudden and unexpected, overwhelming the old overwhelming of suffering. This is the hope the church clings to through all the tribulations of this world.

Until God's kingdom comes on earth, Jesus' parable causes us to scan for signs that this new age is on the way, whether in nature or in the sign of the wood of Calvary budding into new life.

Give us grace to see your sudden kingdom coming. Amen.

ROLAND RIEM

Facing judgement

Then the one who had received the one talent also came forward, saying, 'Master, I knew that you were a harsh man, reaping where you did not sow and gathering where you did not scatter seed, so I was afraid, and I went and hid your talent in the ground. Here you have what is yours.' But his master replied, 'You wicked and lazy slave! You knew, did you, that I reap where I did not sow and gather where I did not scatter?'

If the Son of Man is to return and the familiar world not survive his testing, how should Christ's disciples live today? The parable of the talents builds to the case of the slave with one talent. The slaves with five and two talents to look after have both doubled their money and duly received their master's approval for being good and trustworthy. The slave with one talent – the sort of money it would take a labourer 20 years to earn – is next up.

This third slave does not fare so well. Fear paralyses him and causes him to bury the talent he has been given. As is always the case with fear, it causes him to accentuate the negative: his master is not only harsh, but manifestly unjust, reaping where he did not sow and gathering where he did not scatter.

There is nothing in the story to suggest the master would do this; on the contrary, he is happy to gather proportionately from the slaves with five and two talents, and even to accept banker's interest on the one talent. This master simply acts with good business sense, giving the one talent to the slave who can bring him the greatest return, though his wrath finally falls on the worthless slave.

Jesus' parable channels the irrational fear of accountability back to the question of how we use the generous gifts of God. It does not identify those gifts and it accepts that there will be others with, seemingly, far greater talents than our own. No matter.

Let us pray that God gives us grace to know what our talents are,
at every stage of our lives, and the courage to see
how to make good trade with them.

ROLAND RIEM

Anointed for burial

Now while Jesus was at Bethany in the house of Simon the leper, a woman came to him with an alabaster jar of very costly ointment, and she poured it on his head as he sat at the table… Jesus… said to them… 'By pouring this ointment on my body she has prepared me for burial. Truly I tell you, wherever this good news is proclaimed in the whole world, what she has done will be told in remembrance of her.'

Jesus' anointing at Bethany stands like an oasis of kindness between the episodes of the chief priests and elders planning to kill him and their being given the opportunity to do so by Judas' betrayal. Between them, the shadow of death falls over Jesus and his small band of disciples.

A woman comes into the house where they are staying with 'an alabaster jar of very costly ointment' (v. 7) and a mission to lavish his head with it. When the disciples react against this, Jesus shows his understanding of her intention and of the significance of her act, which anticipates his coming burial. (In Matthew's gospel he does not receive a later anointing at the tomb.)

There is quite a difference between the disciples' reaction, who see the charitable potential in exchanging her offering for cash, and the awareness shared by the unnamed woman and Jesus: this is a special moment, the truth of which is revealed in this prophetic act. Like a parable, it points beyond itself to the kingdom of God.

In rebuking his disciples, Jesus takes us to the heart of what it means to follow him, which is to stand by him and identify with him in his self-sacrificial love for the world. The woman offers costly ointment where soon he will offer costly bread and wine to signify the gift of his life for the restoration of creation.

Although the disciples are portrayed in a positive light in Matthew's gospel as learners, they still have much to learn. Salvation comes not through holding the world at a comfortable, charitable distance, but by standing with Jesus in his suffering. This practical identification with our Saviour will have the profoundest impact on the continuing spiritual and material poverty of the present age.

Reflect on how sharing in Christ's self-sacrificial love is a precious offering.

ROLAND RIEM

The pouring cup

Then he took a cup, and after giving thanks he gave it to them, saying, 'Drink from it, all of you, for this is my blood of the covenant, which is poured out for many for the forgiveness of sins. I tell you, I will never again drink of this fruit of the vine until that day when I drink it new with you in my Father's kingdom.'

Some prophetic actions belong so fully to the routine of worship that it is hard to see them in the light of the coming kingdom. Indeed, Matthew's version of the institution of the Lord's Supper shows signs that Jesus' words at Passover had already been polished by liturgical use.

We also have to set aside medieval disputes about the 'essence' of the Eucharistic bread and wine and how they relate to the actual body and blood of Christ. These focus so much on the eucharistic elements that the story and actions around them, celebrated by the gathered community and holding their essential meaning, can be lost.

In the gospel, Jesus is presiding over a Passover meal with his disciples, in a ritual which looked back to the rescue of God's people at the exodus and looked forward to their final deliverance. He pours the wine into the cup and passes it around, identifying his death for the forgiveness of sins with that earlier deliverance. His blood would extend the covenant made with Israel, as his death would be for 'many'.

His death would change the nature of the covenant meal: no longer an earthly memorial but one presided over from the heavenly realm. When Christians meet to share the cup, they drink with Jesus in his Father's kingdom, so that they share not only in his saving death but also in his final vindication – the sacrificial lamb now upon the throne.

The story as Matthew tells it unites the past (the last supper) with the present worship of his community and with the eternal worship of the heavenly host around God's throne. No wonder that this taking of bread and wine remains the church's defining act, in which Christians find strength and hope by entering the covenant made really present, still being poured out in love for many.

Pray that God's covenant love may flow through us to the thirsty.

ROLAND RIEM

False signs

Jesus was silent. Then the high priest said to him, 'I put you under oath before the living God, tell us if you are the Messiah, the Son of God.' Jesus said to him, 'You have said so. But I tell you, From now on you will see the Son of Man seated at the right hand of Power and coming on the clouds of heaven.' Then the high priest tore his clothes and said, 'He has blasphemed! Why do we still need witnesses? You have now heard his blasphemy.'

The high priest seems as if he is trying to get to the truth when he puts Jesus on oath, but it is as much to put him under pressure to end his silence, as witnesses accuse him of threatening to destroy and then rebuild the temple. The high priest presses to the heart of the issue: is this claim based on who Jesus thinks he is?

Earlier, at Caesarea Philippi, Jesus accepted Peter's confession of him as Messiah and Son of the living God. But as he breaks his silence here, Jesus goes even further than this. He reveals himself as the figure promised in the book of Daniel, the 'Son of Man' to whom God would delegate 'dominion and glory and kingship, that all peoples, nations and languages should serve him' (Daniel 7:14). The high priest and his whole council, who now stand in judgement on God's own Messiah, would one day be judged by him.

While Christ is entirely truthful throughout, the high priest, in tearing his sacred robes, undermines his own authority, breaking the Mosaic law (Leviticus 21:10). Though dramatic, his act is in fact shallow and rhetorical, matching the equally vague accusation of 'blasphemy', which has not been proven, only asserted.

Outrage on social media and in public life by those staking claim to moral authority is commonplace in our own time. Why should we need to be any more prudent than the high priest when we are so blisteringly sure of what is wrong? The authority of Jesus, however, is based on a threefold integrity of word, action and belief. It keeps silence in the face of false accusation and speaks truth bravely. It is an authority hard to recognise and harder still to imitate.

Help us to witness to what lies beyond lies. Amen.

ROLAND RIEM

Body language

When Judas, his betrayer, saw that Jesus was condemned, he repented and brought back the thirty pieces of silver to the chief priests and the elders. He said, 'I have sinned by betraying innocent blood.' But they said, 'What is that to us? See to it yourself.' Throwing down the pieces of silver in the temple, he departed, and he went and hanged himself.

Judas wanted to betray Jesus. Earlier he had gone to the chief priest to ask how much they would give him to betray him. When they agreed on 30 pieces of silver, Judas, shockingly one of the twelve apostles, began to look for an opportunity to do so. Judas is rightly remembered in the Bible and in history as the one who betrayed his master.

The betrayal is followed by regret. The fact that readers of Matthew's story are not given the reasons for Judas' actions only makes its pointlessness stronger. We see by what happens here that the money has been a smokescreen, to give Judas' actions a veneer of reason. What he has done is to sin against God, and for that grave sin, ironically, the priests of the temple show no concern whatever.

When Judas departs from them and goes out to hang himself, away from his co-conspirators, away from the other eleven and his Lord, a parable of judgement is being played out. The 'weeping and gnashing of teeth', reserved for those who forget their wedding garment, translates into this despairing and desolate scene, where a former friend of Jesus swings forlornly from a tree.

Against this bleak body language stands Jesus' innocent blood, reminding us of Abel's blood which, despite the murderous stealth of his brother Cain, cried out to God from the ground. Jesus' innocent blood drove Judas to his death, gripped by the magnitude of his crime.

There is still horror in betrayal, though now we tend to use the word 'abuse' to describe it, a betrayal of trust and relationship with inevitable and devastating consequences. Jesus takes Judas' abuse and all our own abuses, given and received, into his journey to the cross, where he will hang to wrestle something new from the pit of human wickedness.

Your blood avails for me. Amen.

ROLAND RIEM

Blood washing

So when Pilate saw that he could do nothing but rather that a riot was beginning, he took some water and washed his hands before the crowd, saying, 'I am innocent of this man's blood; see to it yourselves.' Then the people as a whole answered, 'His blood be on us and on our children!' So he released Barabbas for them, and after flogging Jesus he handed him over to be crucified.

Judas was unable to rid himself of his blood guilt, but Pilate was more practised at washing his hands of responsibility. Pilate's official residence was on the shores of the Mediterranean, in the Roman capital of Judea, but as governor of the region he was obliged to visit Jerusalem for the major pilgrim festivals, to keep the peace when its swollen population was at its most volatile.

Pilate cares nothing for the dispute between Jesus and the religious authorities, and he cannot make sense of the so-called King of the Jews. He realises, though, that Jesus is no threat to peace. Pilate finds a way to diffuse the situation by using the Roman custom of releasing a prisoner at Passover: a win–win to satisfy Jewish unrest with Roman clemency.

Pilate's offer only inflames the crowd, who insist on a freedom fighter's release rather than Jesus'. So Pilate washes his hands of the matter, judging himself innocent before the assembly; and we watch in horror as the guilt for Jesus' blood passes from Pilate to the whole people of God, who shout willingly, 'His blood be on us and on our children!'

In AD70, less than two generations after Jesus' execution, the temple built by King Herod would be destroyed. Matthew and other Christians saw this as judgement on God's ancient, beloved people for their rejection of their King.

Though they deserted Jesus, the King of the Jews did not desert them. His blood shed from the cross cried out for mercy on the many surviving Jerusalem's destruction. Some of these dispersed people of Judea found themselves driven north, living among Gentiles in Syria, and it was probably there that Matthew's community offered good news – to Gentile, Jew and all nations, and a baptism for the washing away of sins.

Wash us, for we cannot wash our own hands clean. Amen.

ROLAND RIEM

Real kingship

And when they came to a place called Golgotha (which means Place of a Skull), they offered him wine to drink, mixed with gall, but when he tasted it, he would not drink it. And when they had crucified him, they divided his clothes among themselves by casting lots; then they sat down there and kept watch over him. Over his head they put the charge against him, which read, 'This is Jesus, the King of the Jews.'

God's rule began before Jesus was born. We see this from the beginning of Matthew's gospel, in the pattern of 3 x 14 generations leading up to Jesus' birth. This is a pattern of God working in and through events, taking in both the good (such as King David's anointing) and the bad (such as national exile) along the way.

Jesus announced God's kingdom and was its emissary. He lived every moment tuned in to his Father's will, in both the good times and the bad. The events leading to the crucifixion counted as the very worst of times, at least on the surface of things. God's work and will, however, ran through these events, not around them.

There is nothing to stop the thuggery of the occupying army: soldiers driving a thorny crown on to Jesus' head, spitting and striking him, offering him gall-poison, crucifying him, gambling for his clothing and mocking him further with a notice proclaiming a condemned criminal as king.

Everything, though, is following a deeper pattern prophesied in scripture. For example, the giving of poison alludes to Psalm 69:21, and the division of garments to Psalm 22:18. And eventually when Jesus dies on the cross, his cry of dereliction does justice to his total abandonment, while also being a fulfilment of Psalm 22:1: 'My God, my God, why have you forsaken me?'

Magical kingship – the sort all who mock and taunt Jesus want – means stepping off the cross and avoiding suffering. True kingship means suffering the work of God in the worst of times, trusting that God is working secretly in and through the long hours of darkness. At this crucial point, it is all that Jesus needs to do, and all that he can do.

Always hang on in there, with Christ the true King.

ROLAND RIEM

The curtain torn

When some of the bystanders heard it, they said, 'This man is calling for Elijah.' At once one of them ran and got a sponge, filled it with sour wine, put it on a stick, and gave it to him to drink. But the others said, 'Wait, let us see whether Elijah will come to save him.' Then Jesus cried again with a loud voice and breathed his last. At that moment the curtain of the temple was torn in two, from top to bottom.

The bystanders at the crucifixion, wanting a good show, speculate on what might happen after Jesus' cry of dereliction. One of them, wanting to hear more, goes off to find something to parch Jesus' thirst, and in so doing fulfils more of Psalm 69:21: 'For my thirst they gave me vinegar to drink.' Others, misunderstanding Jesus to be calling for Elijah rather than God, wait for any sign that the prophet might show up and kick something off.

But Jesus is not saved by either God or Elijah; Jesus cries again with a loud voice and breathes his last. John will make more of this in the fourth gospel, but clearly Jesus is not leaving this world with a whimper. He means to die. He knows that he must give up his spirit, and it is possible too that this loud cry heralds the age to come, along with a series of signs and wonders.

The first sign is that the temple curtain is torn from top to bottom, anticipating the destruction of the temple. It is God who tears it and God who by tearing it vindicates his Son Jesus, who said that he would destroy the temple and build it in three days. Jesus was meant to die, but beyond death comes a cluster of signs to show that God was there with him all along, working through his passion.

Jesus' death is revealed as the ultimate parable of passion, a story with a mighty twist, with urgent mystery, revealed in signs hidden from speculating bystanders. Can we rather hear the parable, see what has been achieved and follow the centurion's awed confession: 'Truly this was [and still is for us today] the Son of God?' (see Matthew 27:54).

God, tear down whatever stands before your glory. Amen.

ROLAND RIEM

'He has risen!' Practising resurrection

 The season of Easter, which we've now entered, should be one of joy, feasting and the drinking of a lot of bubbly – so says the theologian Tom Wright. I agree. Many of us have come to observe the season of Lent with fasting and self-examination, but we lose out when we do not enjoy the spiritual practice of celebration. And we have the best news to rejoice over – Jesus lives! He did not stay dead! The resurrection is real! Alleluia!

As we explore the story of the resurrection this week through the synoptic gospels, Matthew, Mark and Luke, we see how it is one of contrasts – surprise, shock and disbelief along with wonder, celebration and overflowing joy. For instance, the way the women, when Jesus appears to them, believe straight away differs from the men, who take longer to understand that Jesus really is alive and has a resurrected body. Thus if we hold a lurking feeling that we should react to these stories in a particular way or by a certain timeline, we can find encouragement by the varied responses. God understands that we may come to know and believe in his resurrected life according to our own personality and volition.

During this season and beyond we can, in the words of the poet Wendell Berry, practise resurrection. When we do so daily, we stand against hopelessness and despair. We recognise the glories of our Creator God, who formed us in his image. We acknowledge that the risen Christ may appear in our lives in unexpected and amazing ways. And we collaborate with the indwelling Spirit, who empowers us to love the needy, work for justice, forgive those who repent, extend kindness to the awkward and walk with our God day by day.

This week I invite you to notice how Jesus may break through and surprise you. Perhaps you will receive an act of kindness from a stranger, or enjoy the best night of sleep in a long time, or delight at the smile of a child. When we ask God to show us how he is at work, we will see more and more the evidence of his resurrection power. Not least in how we seek to live each day.

AMY BOUCHER PYE

Earth-shattering news

When the Sabbath was over, Mary Magdalene, Mary the mother of James, and Salome bought spices so that they might go to anoint Jesus' body. Very early on the first day of the week, just after sunrise, they were on their way to the tomb and they asked each other, 'Who will roll the stone away from the entrance of the tomb?'... There was a violent earthquake, for an angel of the Lord came down from heaven and, going to the tomb, rolled back the stone and sat on it. His appearance was like lightning, and his clothes were white as snow. The guards were so afraid of him that they shook and became like dead men.

'Christ is risen! He is risen indeed! Alleluia!' This refrain will echo around the world today as Christians express their joy over the good news of Jesus – he who died yet lives. But as we rejoice, take a few moments to put yourselves in the sandals of the women who discovered the empty tomb.

Weighed down with grief after their friend was killed, they wanted to care for his broken body. But they could not buy the anointing spices until the sabbath was over and the new day dawned. Spices in hand, in a fog of grief, they made their way to the tomb and realised that the stone would be too heavy to move. How shattering that must have felt – they who wanted to pour out their love in the only practical way available were stymied in their quest.

Then consider their great surprise when God intervened with the earth shaking and an angel appearing to do the heavy lifting. This unexpected turn of events, with the blazing-bright appearance of this angel, must have shaken off the weariness of their deep grief. The women stay alert while the guards can't handle the shock, their bodies closing down.

What a joy for us that God continues to burst on to the scene. If we feel weighed down in an impenetrable fog, we can trust that he can send the light of his Spirit to dispel the clouds. Jesus is alive!

Risen Christ, you weren't contained by the tomb! You are risen! Alleluia!

AMY BOUCHER PYE

Divine passive

In their fright the women bowed down with their faces to the ground, but the men said to them, 'Why do you look for the living among the dead? He is not here; he has risen! Remember how he told you, while he was still with you in Galilee: "The Son of Man must be delivered over to the hands of sinners, be crucified and on the third day be raised again."' Then they remembered his words.

Because of its vitality, I love using the active tense when writing. But I also love what is known as the 'divine passive', and that is what we see in this passage. It appears just after the angel asks the women why they are looking for the living in a grave; as they say, 'He is not here; he has risen!' In the Greek, the latter part of that sentence is more accurately translated 'He has been raised!' The angel delivers this stunning news, and the grammar points to God as the one who made it happen.

The women hardly have time to ponder what this means when the angel reminds them what Jesus said previously – that after being killed he would be raised again to life.

It is easy to overlook the wonder of God sharing this miracle with *women* first. Many rabbis would not trust women to be witnesses. Women received no education and were not allowed to read the Torah, the scriptures, or even touch them. All of their learning would have been done via their fathers, husbands or rabbis. Yet God revealed that his Son was alive to those from this less-valued segment of society, going against the expectations of that culture. For God is not limited by what humans create.

On this Easter Monday, why not take some time to ponder the upside-down kingdom of Jesus, including that he died but did not stay dead, that lowly women, not rulers and kings, heard the news first, and the many other wonders that God brings about, including in our own lives.

Saving God, thank you for how you break into our hearts and minds. Open me to receive from you in whatever form you choose. Amen.

AMY BOUCHER PYE

On a mission

'Then go quickly and tell his disciples: "He has risen from the dead and is going ahead of you into Galilee. There you will see him." Now I have told you.' So the women hurried away from the tomb, afraid yet filled with joy, and ran to tell his disciples. Suddenly Jesus met them. 'Greetings,' he said. They came to him, clasped his feet and worshipped him. Then Jesus said to them, 'Do not be afraid. Go and tell my brothers to go to Galilee; there they will see me.'

What a whirlwind for the women. Tasked with sharing the shocking news that their friend was not dead but alive, they reverberated with not only joy but trepidation. They would have felt that stomach-churning anticipation of sharing a big announcement when one does not know how everything will turn out. The closest I can imagine was sharing the news that my husband and I were expecting a baby.

The women's emotions would have been rocked even more when none other than Jesus himself appeared to them! Note how they fell down immediately to worship, grabbing on to his feet – that detail would have lodged in the minds of the original audience, indicating that this was not a spirit-only resurrection. After all, Jesus had feet that they could clasp.

The place mentioned by the angel and Jesus is important too – Galilee. This was the main space for Jesus' ministry; his friends, whom he calls his brothers, would know where to meet him. Also, that he does not specify Jerusalem as the meeting place underscores that he comes not only for Jewish people but Gentiles too.

Jesus loves these women and treats them with respect. He tasks them with sharing the extraordinary news of him being alive, all the while giving them reassurance and telling them not to fear. The risen Christ continues to love and affirm us, and also gives us the mission of sharing his good news. Perhaps today you will sense a nudge with his loving invitation to partner with him.

Living Lord, help me to receive your presence. Thank you for entrusting me with collaborating with you. Equip me to do your will, with love. Amen.

AMY BOUCHER PYE

Invitation to believe

When they came back from the tomb, they told all these things to the Eleven and to all the others. It was Mary Magdalene, Joanna, Mary the mother of James, and the others with them who told this to the apostles. But they did not believe the women, because their words seemed to them like nonsense. Peter, however, got up and ran to the tomb. Bending over, he saw the strips of linen lying by themselves, and he went away, wondering to himself what had happened.

Jesus appeared in bodily form, but the men did not believe it. Their reaction, in fact, was not only disbelief; they also thought the women spoke nonsense. How difficult for these faithful female disciples, those who went to anoint Jesus' body and ended up witnessing a miracle. Now the men questioned their words.

Notice Peter, however. He had been humbled by his denial of Jesus, which Jesus had foretold. Perhaps his heart became tender as he realised that he did not always grasp the full story. Going on his own search of the tomb, he saw no body but glimpsed the strips of linen that Jesus was buried in. And he wondered what this all meant. Many scholars read this negatively, assuming that he still doubted, but some see this as an opening to faith and belief. That reading of the text seems more likely to me, too. I prefer to think that Peter learned from betraying Jesus, and he pondered with hope the mystery of Jesus actually being alive.

Belief can come in a flash, but it can be a journey too. When first the angel and then Jesus visited the women, they had instant opportunities to believe. Peter, in contrast, had longer to process, which perhaps is what he needed as he restored his hope in the Saviour.

As those who follow Christ, we are called to believe. Sometimes this feels the hardest thing to do – to extend our faith when people, circumstances and institutions all seem to work against us. At these times we can remember the women and Peter and how they came to believe, knowing that God can change our hearts too.

Living Jesus, I believe; help my unbelief. Amen.

AMY BOUCHER PYE

Journeying with Jesus

**Now that same day two of them were going to a village called Emmaus…
Jesus himself came up and walked along with them; but they were kept
from recognising him. He asked them, 'What are you discussing together
as you walk along?'… 'About Jesus of Nazareth,' they replied. 'He was a
prophet, powerful in word and deed before God and all the people. The
chief priests and our rulers handed him over to be sentenced to death,
and they crucified him; but we had hoped that he was the one who was
going to redeem Israel… In addition, some of our women amazed us. They
went to the tomb early this morning but didn't find his body. They came
and told us that they had seen a vision of angels, who said he was alive.'**

Two disciples walked along a road, dejected. Jesus had disappointed them
and had not ushered in a new era of political influence. When he hung on
the cross, their hopes were dashed. As Cleopas and his friend (who could
have been his wife) debriefed all that they had seen and heard, they tried
to make sense of it. But no sense could be found as they circled around the
'what ifs' and the 'why nots'.

Yet God broke through, just as earlier when Jesus appeared to the women
by the tomb. Interestingly, God did not allow these travellers to know right
away that they were in the presence of the resurrected Christ. Perhaps
he wanted them to be able to share with him who they thought he was
(note – a prophet, not the Messiah) and how desperate they felt over his
death. Their perplexed questions reveal their feelings and thoughts: dejec-
tion, pain and confused amazement at what the women said. They simply
could not work it all out.

Perhaps we too circle round with our questions, doubts and concerns. But
Jesus does not leave us alone on our journeys of faith. He comes alongside
us and allows us to express everything that baffles us, showing up perhaps
when we least expect it. He lives in and among us.

*Living Lord, open my eyes to see you. Help me to be aware of your presence
and give me your peace. Amen.*

AMY BOUCHER PYE

It is true!

He said to them, 'How foolish you are, and how slow to believe all that the prophets have spoken! Did not the Messiah have to suffer these things and then enter his glory?' And beginning with Moses and all the Prophets, he explained to them what was said in all the Scriptures concerning himself… They urged him strongly, 'Stay with us'… When he was at the table with them, he took bread, gave thanks, broke it and began to give it to them. Then their eyes were opened and they recognised him, and he disappeared from their sight… They found the Eleven and those with them, assembled together and saying, 'It is true! The Lord has risen and has appeared to Simon.'

What a Bible study that must have been, when Jesus led his friends through the scriptures, starting with Moses and moving through the Old Testament promises of the coming Messiah. But he first exhorted them over their disbelief. Although he hoped they would have figured out his true identity after all the time they had spent with him, he did not withhold from them the glorious message of how Jesus fulfilled the promises of God. Through this discussion, they still did not realise that he was speaking about himself. Only later when they were gathered in the setting of a meal, breaking bread together, were their eyes opened.

Notice the main message of Jesus, how he had to suffer before entering glory. God's redemption plan for humanity involved this sequence of events; the suffering of the chosen one was required. Remembering that Jesus did not shirk from the ultimate sacrifice can help us when we baulk over the challenging things we face. We can also seek from him the strength and hope to endure.

After the disciples understood that it really was Jesus, their weight of grief evaporated and they turned right around and headed back the seven miles to Jerusalem to share their joy with the others. Because Jesus appeared to them, they too believed. He appears to us too, and we also can believe and rejoice.

Living Jesus, I welcome your presence in my life. Help me to discern how in you I live and move and have my being.

AMY BOUCHER PYE

Power from on high

While they were still talking about this, Jesus himself stood among them and said to them, 'Peace be with you.' They were startled and frightened, thinking they saw a ghost. He said to them, 'Why are you troubled…? Look at my hands and my feet. It is I myself! Touch me and see; a ghost does not have flesh and bones, as you see I have'… He said to them, 'This is what I told you while I was still with you: everything must be fulfilled that is written about me in the law of Moses, the prophets and the psalms.' Then he opened their minds so they could understand the scriptures… You are witnesses of these things. I am going to send you what my Father has promised; but stay in the city until you have been clothed with power from on high.'

The unfolding of the resurrection continued when Jesus appeared to the disciples who had just welcomed back Cleopas and his companion. Instead of hearing the witness of these two travellers only, the gathered group found themselves meeting the resurrected Lord himself. But they did not let themselves believe it was him until he ate broiled fish in their presence – then they understood that he wasn't some kind of wispy spirit, but that he had a real resurrected body. Again Jesus opened the scriptures, highlighting the golden threads in their sacred texts that revealed him as the promised Saviour, the Messiah.

Jesus knew that they needed the Spirit to help them share the good news of his life, death and resurrection. Thus he instructed them to stay in Jerusalem until they received their new set of clothes, those infused with the power from on high.

Jesus does not have to curtail us as he did those gathered and ask us to wait; living after Pentecost, we receive the Spirit when we believe in Jesus. We can now embrace a resurrected life, one filled with God's gracious presence through the Spirit of Jesus who dwells within. In doing so we collaborate with God in the spreading of his kingdom through our loving words and actions.

Father, Son and Spirit, I praise you for this resurrection story. Help me to live out its wonderful promises each day. Amen.

AMY BOUCHER PYE

Alive in Christ: 1 Corinthians 15—16

We enter the second week of Easter today, 7 April, and continue to celebrate the 40-day festival until we reach Ascension Day on 9 May and Pentecost ten days later. It is a season that perfectly counterbalances the 40 days of Lent, as we move from the focus on temptations and sin, the cross and Christ's sacrifice for the world, to that of Christ raised to new life, meeting us with words of peace, sending us out in his name, to bring hope, joy and love to a broken world.

Christians are called to be Easter people, made alive in Christ, the opposite to dull routine or joyless duty. To be Easter people we need to take the risen Christ to heart, to take the risk of faith in the resurrection, not only of Jesus, but of ourselves. To help us do that it is good to turn to the great 15th chapter of Paul's first letter to the Corinthians.

This letter was part of a correspondence between Paul and the church he had helped to establish. Much of the correspondence has been lost, but what has been preserved in the two New Testament letters gives a deep insight into Paul's faith and his work with a Christian community that wrestled with many questions and challenges in a culture often at odds with the way of Jesus.

The letter takes us on a journey, with great mountaintop moments and deep dark valleys. Yet for all its twists and turns, Paul holds on to the reality of Jesus Christ, crucified Saviour and risen Lord. That is the heart of his faith and our faith, the reason for hope and the inspirer of love. The letter reaches the very heights in chapter 15, as Paul shares the mystery and wonder of Christ's resurrection and that 'in Christ shall all be made alive'. If this was a musical composition that is where many would have stopped, but Paul takes us back down to earth in the final chapter as he reaffirms the ordinary work of Jesus' followers – the collections to help those facing famine, the visits of fellow Christians to support and encourage, the greetings sent from one person to the next.

TERRY HINKS

Can I remind you?

Now, brothers and sisters, I want to remind you of the gospel I preached to you, which you received and on which you have taken your stand. By this gospel you are saved, if you hold firmly to the word I preached to you. Otherwise, you have believed in vain.

How many reminders do you have in your house? Reminders to take out the right bins on a particular day, the list of shopping you need, the dates and times of appointments, visits or special plans? Or if not reminders of things to do, then reminders of people and special celebrations – a wedding photo, a certificate or trophy, a gift from a special friend, a treasured heirloom?

We all need reminders, and here in this crucial chapter Paul reminds the Christian community in Corinth of the good news that he had himself received and shared when he was staying with them – the good news that had such an impact on their lives then, and which he hopes and prays will continue to do so now and in the years ahead.

This is more than a gentle reminder; it is a heartfelt plea not to forget, not to lose touch with the very heart of the good news of Jesus Christ, their crucified Saviour and risen Lord. This is the message that they received like a precious gift, the message on which they stand or fall as followers of Jesus, the message through which they are being saved.

'Being saved' is not a done deal. It is a process in which we are caught up, as we follow Jesus and take his amazing compassion and grace to heart, living it out day by day. The journey is not without risks and challenges. We can lose touch with the real Jesus and construct a more comfortable story of our own, a faith that is not active in love or a love that turns inward. Constantly we have to turn to the living Lord, the true Jesus who leads us on, and on whom we rely to be found and rescued.

Thank God today for the good news of Jesus, whether the day be easy or hard.

TERRY HINKS

Passing on the greatest news

For I handed on to you as of first importance what I in turn had received: that Christ died for our sins in accordance with the scriptures and that he was buried and that he was raised on the third day in accordance with the scriptures and that he appeared to Cephas, then to the twelve. Then he appeared to more than five hundred brothers and sisters at one time, most of whom are still alive, though some have died. Then he appeared to James, then to all the apostles.

Objects handed on from one generation to another have great power, linking to family experiences and people of the past. The popular BBC TV series *The Repair Shop* brings together families with stories to tell and an object to repair, with skilled craftspeople whose work is not simply to repair but also to listen. The resulting impact on the objects and the families is moving to watch.

Paul has some crucial and foundational stories about Jesus to pass on to his friends at Corinth. Earlier in the letter he shared how on the night of his arrest, Jesus took bread and wine, said distinctive words linking these simple gifts to his coming sacrifice on the cross and then shared them with his disciples. Now in this chapter he shares the great story of Jesus' sacrificial death for all, his burial, his mighty resurrection 'on the third day' and his appearances to different groups of disciples, turning their grief into joy, their guilt into freedom. Alongside the personal encounters for Peter and James and the inner group of the twelve disciples, there is the great communal experience of over 500 followers, an event that is not recorded in the four gospels but must have been an extraordinary experience.

For Paul these are the fundamental facts of faith that he received and passed on to new followers of Jesus. They have the power to transform people, from the inside out. The wonderful thing about this story is that, unlike an object, handing it on does not involve losing it. It multiplies with the telling and has done so down the centuries. How will we pass it on to those around us today?

Reflect on where you stand in the continuing story of Jesus Christ.

TERRY HINKS

Getting personal

Last of all, as to one untimely born, he appeared also to me. For I am the least of the apostles, unfit to be called an apostle, because I persecuted the church of God. But by the grace of God I am what I am, and his grace towards me has not been in vain. On the contrary, I worked harder than any of them, though it was not I, but the grace of God that is with me. Whether then it was I or they, so we proclaim and so you believed.

Paul began his reflection by sharing the fundamental message he had received and passed on – the inheritance of the faith that we too have received and are called to hand on. Now he moves to his own experience of the risen Jesus. He knows that it is different to those of the first apostles and disciples in Jerusalem, but he also knows it to be equally valid and life-changing. He too had met the risen Lord, not in those first critical days, so soon after the crucifixion of Jesus, but in a visionary experience on the road to Damascus. Far from coming when he was part of the Christian community, he was confronted with the reality of Christ at a moment when he was most fiercely opposed to the whole Jesus movement.

Here was the persecutor turned into the humble follower, the enemy of the church turned into a friend of Jesus. No wonder he talks of himself as 'someone untimely born'. He came to believe in Jesus, despite himself.

Few of us can claim to have such a dramatic encounter with Christ as this. Yet that same risen Jesus meets us today in the joys and heartaches of life. As the famous theologian and missionary Albert Schweitzer described so beautifully, Jesus comes and calls us to the tasks he wants to fulfil here and now. Paul's encounter with Christ set him to work, travelling across the Mediterranean to share good news with people of many backgrounds. That was his task – and he can say, 'By the grace of God I am what I am' (v. 10).

Be yourself today – but be yourself filled and inspired by the grace of God.

TERRY HINKS

How can you?

Now if Christ is proclaimed as raised from the dead, how can some of you say there is no resurrection of the dead? If there is no resurrection of the dead, then Christ has not been raised, and if Christ has not been raised, then our proclamation is in vain and your faith is in vain... If for this life only we have hoped in Christ, we are of all people most to be pitied.

Imagine listening in on someone's phone conversation. 'You what?' you hear the person exclaim, and then, 'No, really? You can't be serious.' You long for the person to put the phone on speaker mode to hear what the other person is saying. We hear the same shocked tone here, as Paul responds to the report that some of the Corinthian Christians do not believe in the resurrection of the dead and expect nothing beyond this life.

We do not know who reported that to Paul or what the exact situation was in Corinth. We know that there was a live debate in Judaism between the Pharisees and the Sadducees, the latter rejecting the idea of resurrection. Paul is astonished to find the debate alive in Christianity too.

For Paul our future is bound up with Jesus. At the cross it seemed that his future was obliterated, yet Paul's experience and the Christian experience is that, far from being the end of Jesus, it was just the beginning. His resurrection in that amazing Easter event brings all humanity the possibility of resurrection to new life.

Equally if there is no resurrection for humanity then it would follow that Jesus himself was not raised. For Paul it works in both directions. Jesus is not God pretending to be human and so easily able to slip past death; Jesus is truly human and so subject to real suffering and real dying. Yet God raised him to life, a promise we can hold for ourselves too.

That is the good news, that is the faith. All of us at times struggle to trust that promise for ourselves and for others, but to succumb to a faith without resurrection is to opt for a lifeless faith that is empty, useless, hopeless and vain.

Lord, I believe. Help my unbelief.

TERRY HINKS

Made alive in Christ

But in fact Christ has been raised from the dead, the first fruits of those who have died. For since death came through a human, the resurrection of the dead has also come through a human, for as all die in Adam, so all will be made alive in Christ. But each in his own order: Christ the first fruits, then at his coming those who belong to Christ. Then comes the end, when he hands over the kingdom to God the Father.

Great songs and poetry take us on a journey of thought and feeling. Paul does the same in this glorious chapter. In the previous verses he reaches the rock bottom of imagining a Christian faith without a risen Lord, drawing out the sense of meaninglessness and hopelessness that this entails. It reminds me of the hymn 'Think of a world without any flowers', which the much-loved Christian teacher Bunty Newport created with children from Emmanuel Church, Cambridge, in the 1960s.

We reach a similar bleak point with Paul, but then he turns the tables with the bold statement that begins 'But in fact', or literally 'But now'. There is no more need to think of being pitied for a faith without power, as we can say together, 'Christ has been raised from the dead.' This is the reality in which we live in our 21st-century world with all its secular influences, different faiths, ideas and philosophies. It is the Christian promise held out not to a select few but to all humanity. In Adam (humanity as it is) all die, but in Christ (symbol and first of the new humanity) all will be made alive – and truly alive with the 'life full to overflowing' that Jesus promised (see John 10:10).

There is a story from the Soviet era in Russia of a Communist speaker denouncing all religious faith to a crowd of peasants gathered in a village square. His arguments for atheism were powerful and he felt pleased with his efforts. But an old Orthodox priest stepped forward and shouted out, 'Christ is risen,' and as one the villagers responded, 'He is risen indeed.'

Ponder what it means to be 'alive in Christ'.

TERRY HINKS

Death destroyed

The last enemy to be destroyed is death. For 'God has put all things in subjection under his feet.' But when it says, 'All things are put in subjection', it is plain that this does not include the one who put all things in subjection under him. When all things are subjected to him, then the Son himself will also be subjected to the one who put all things in subjection under him, so that God may be all in all. Otherwise, what will those people do who receive baptism on behalf of the dead? If the dead are not raised at all, why are people baptised on their behalf?

The 17th-century mystical poet John Donne ends his poem 'Death, be not proud' with the words 'Death, thou shalt die', echoing Paul's theme of death itself being destroyed. We know that death is a fundamental fact of human existence. We hear of deaths reported every day in the media, through illness, accident, disaster, violence and warfare. We try to look the other way and to seek reassurance and comfort where we can. The idea of living on in the genes of the next generation or in the memories of those 'left behind' offers comfort to some. Others look to science to extend life more and more (given enough money). Yet the reality of death remains, seemingly invincible.

From a human perspective that may be true, but it does not reckon with the divine reality, the God who is the source of life and creator of all, and the Son who has overcome death and conquered time and space. The risen Christ becomes Lord over all (even death), though always in loving and humble relationship to God the Father.

Then comes the strange note of people being baptised on behalf of those who have died. This is not a practice that Christians would undertake today. It would seem to undermine the place of choice and faith and commitment in the act of being baptised. We have to recognise that the culture of the early Corinthian church was different from our own. We are not saved by baptism, but by the Saviour. It is his victory over death that matters – for baptised and unbaptised alike.

Pray for those facing death today.

TERRY HINKS

That's a good saying

If I fought with wild animals at Ephesus with a merely human perspective, what would I have gained by it? If the dead are not raised, 'Let us eat and drink, for tomorrow we die.' Do not be deceived: 'Bad company ruins good morals.' Sober up, as you rightly ought to, and sin no more, for some people have no knowledge of God. I say this to your shame.

What proverbs did you learn as a child? Perhaps a family saying or the words of one of your heroes or a fictional character. Lots come to my mind, but the one that I have often thought about is: 'Sticks and stones may break my bones, but words will never hurt me.' I remember walking home from school, saying those words to myself and realising that they were not true for me: words can be very powerful and hurtful indeed.

Paul drew on sayings and proverbs both from his reading of the Hebrew scriptures and Jewish tradition, but also from the surrounding Roman and Greek cultures. He echoes the thoughts of Ecclesiastes to speak of a life without hope beyond death with a quote noted in Isaiah 22:13. Such a life would have no ultimate meaning or purpose beyond simple survival and pleasure. 'Eat, drink and be merry' remains a saying today, though we may prefer to ignore the 'for tomorrow we die'.

Alongside this scriptural quote from the rather gloomy Jewish philosopher comes another from a more secular source: 'Bad company ruins good morals' (v. 33). Paul is happy to speak the language of the day and connect to the culture that is familiar to his Corinthian readers. Whether he knew the quote because it was used far and wide or because he had heard the actual words in the comedy *Thaïs*, written by Athenian dramatist Menander, Paul brought it into what we regard as holy scripture.

So think of that proverb and what kind of company you keep in your social life, your reading and following of social media, the television programmes you watch and the politicians you support. Are you keeping the best company or allowing humanity's worst to ruin your thinking and your following of the best companion, Jesus Christ.

What sayings have influenced you? Are they true?

TERRY HINKS

Fruitful seed

But someone will ask, 'How are the dead raised? With what kind of body do they come?' Fool! What you sow does not come to life unless it dies. And as for what you sow, you do not sow the body that is to be, but a bare seed, perhaps of wheat or of some other grain... So it is with the resurrection of the dead. What is sown is perishable; what is raised is imperishable. It is sown in dishonour; it is raised in glory. It is sown in weakness; it is raised in power. It is sown a physical body; it is raised a spiritual body.

There is an old tradition of sowing potatoes on Good Friday. It is somewhat unscientific, given that the date of Good Friday can vary from 20 March to 23 April. Still there is always something wonderful about burying the small tubers and then finding a week or two later green shoots springing out of the soil (and still later digging over the soil to find a mass of new potatoes). It echoes Jesus' words about his own death, where he says that the seed remains alone unless it is buried and dies, but 'if it dies it bears much fruit' (John 12:24).

Paul uses that image as he speaks about the continuity and discontinuity between this life and the next. He explores in many verses the different kinds of bodies in the world and universe, glorying in the variety of God's creation – from the smallest of animals to the moon and stars. One can imagine Paul delighting in the world around him, while knowing of another country, a spiritual or heavenly realm.

For us all, the hope for this life and beyond is of a growing into the likeness of Christ. In death the seed of our lives is raised by God into life transformed and glorified – like a glorious plant rises from a tiny seed. Death is not to be underestimated – the sowing of this perishable weak life is hard, but God's raising of our lives is glorious and powerful and eternal. Dust is turned to heaven, as we are transformed into the image of Christ, 'the man of heaven'.

What questions would you want to ask Paul about the resurrection?

TERRY HINKS

God gives us the victory!

When this perishable body puts on imperishability and this mortal body puts on immortality, then the saying that is written will be fulfilled: 'Death has been swallowed up in victory.' 'Where, O death, is your victory? Where, O death, is your sting?' The sting of death is sin, and the power of sin is the law. But thanks be to God, who gives us the victory through our Lord Jesus Christ. Therefore, my beloved brothers and sisters, be steadfast, immovable, always excelling in the work of the Lord because you know that in the Lord your labour is not in vain.

What is the great battle in your life? Many feel life to be a struggle, perhaps a battle with inner demons, a fight for survival, a war against illness, a conflict with other powers or a duel with the devil. As far as the contest with death is concerned, it seems a battle that cannot be won. Death is just that one certainty (alongside taxes) that confronts us all.

Paul knows differently. He has wrestled with the wild animals of Ephesus, been imprisoned, beaten, stoned and threatened with execution. He has been betrayed by friends and learned to live with his 'thorn in the flesh' (1 Corinthians 12:7). Paul has seen death close at hand, but now knows the one who has died and is risen.

So, he ends his great chapter on our resurrection by proclaiming *victory*. It is an affirmation of faith, not of sight or certainty, but a bold, honest and true affirmation all the same. Victory has been won by the God of life, through Jesus Christ. Death's sting has been drawn and death will now die. The raising of Jesus Christ into the eternal glory of God means death cannot win the war. The battle will continue – and there will be losses and gains – but there is no question that the war is won.

In that hope, we can live with heads lifted high, determined to play our part in God's transforming, life-giving work. We can join Paul and all who have gone before us in saying, 'Thanks be to God, who gives us the victory through our Lord Jesus Christ'.

'Thine be the glory, risen, conqu'ring Son, endless is the vict'ry thou o'er death hast won' (Edmond Budry, 1854–1932).

TERRY HINKS

And now we'll take up the collection!

Now concerning the collection for the saints: you should follow the directions I gave to the churches of Galatia. On the first day of every week, each of you is to put aside and save whatever extra you earn, so that collections need not be taken when I come. And when I arrive, I will send any whom you approve with letters to take your gift to Jerusalem. If it seems advisable that I should go also, they will accompany me.

Now we move from the majestic to the mundane, from the victory of the risen Christ to the church collection. It feels a bit of a let down, like those moments when the congregation is captivated by a sense of worship and suddenly the audio-visual system packs up and people are scurrying round trying to fix things!

Nevertheless it is good that we have this chapter to consider alongside the previous magnificent one. We cannot stay on a spiritual high for too long. It is like Jesus and his disciples coming down from the mountain to get on with the work he was called to do among the ordinary people of his time. Paul knows there is work to do, and he ends his reflection on the victory of the risen Christ by connecting this with the work the Corinthian Christians were doing. Their witnessing, serving, praying and caring were all given hope and purpose through that eternal life Christ had won for them.

So let us get down to 'brass tacks', to see whether money matches mouths. Paul gives careful instructions so that this collection is well thought out and properly prepared, rather than a last-minute rush when he arrives. His offer here to accompany those taking the gift all the way to Jerusalem was taken up, and it ultimately led to his being imprisoned and then taken to Rome. There he was held under house arrest and, according to tradition, ultimately died a martyr's death. The collection was that important to him. It is a challenge to us to reflect carefully on what needs we are being called to meet and to give generously today.

'Take my life and let it be, consecrated, Lord, to thee'
(Frances Havergal, 1836–79).

TERRY HINKS

Giving time

I will visit you after passing through Macedonia – for I intend to pass through Macedonia – and perhaps I will stay with you or even spend the winter, so that you may send me on my way, wherever I go. I do not want to see you now just in passing, for I hope to spend some time with you, if the Lord permits. But I will stay in Ephesus until Pentecost, for a wide door for effective work has opened to me, and there are many adversaries.

The Covid-19 pandemic caused huge disruption to people's lives across the world. Plans were cancelled or put on hold, weddings were rearranged and then rearranged again, and travelling any distance or visiting family became impossible. We discovered new ways of connecting online, but there was still a great sense of loss and, for many, real anxiety and fear.

Paul lived in uncertain times too, and while he shares his travel plans and hopes to visit the Corinthian church, he does not take those plans for granted. He wants and hopes to see them 'if the Lord permits' (v. 7). For him, all relies on the grace and providence of God.

What is clear is that Paul believes it is important to give people time. He does not just want to call in on Corinth, to pay them a passing visit. He wants to stay long enough to embed himself once more among his troublesome friends there, to listen and speak, heart to heart. Equally he is staying on in Ephesus because his work there is bearing fruit; there is a 'wide door' (v. 9). He is waiting until Pentecost – a rare mention by Paul of a Jewish religious festival – but one associated with the first harvest and then in the church with the empowering work of the Holy Spirit.

How do we use our time? Do we give other people the time they need or do we skate over the surface? Are we willing to go deeper? To face the real questions of life, to listen to their hopes and dreams, so often left unexpressed?

God of every season, thank you for the gift of time.
May I use my time wisely, generously, graciously,
knowing the right time to do, to be and to pray. Amen.

TERRY HINKS

Valued friends

If Timothy comes, see that he has nothing to fear among you, for he is doing the work of the Lord just as I am; therefore let no one despise him. Send him on his way in peace, so that he may come to me, for I am expecting him with the brothers and sisters. Now concerning our brother Apollos, I strongly urged him to visit you with the other brothers and sisters, but he was not at all willing to come now. He will come when he has the opportunity. Keep alert; stand firm in your faith; be courageous; be strong. Let all that you do be done in love.

Now we turn from the work Paul wants to do to the people he works with, those who share the calling to teach the gospel. Timothy is mentioned in many of Paul's letters, a trusted companion who was often sent to act on Paul's behalf. The task Timothy has in Corinth is more difficult than most, so Paul urges the Corinthian readers to take care of him and not look down on him because of his youth or nervousness or inexperience. Paul is clearly protective of Timothy and is looking forward to seeing him before long 'with the brothers and sisters' (v. 11).

For Paul, Christians are both members of the body of Christ and brothers and sisters in Christ. A bond has been formed, as deep or deeper than any blood tie. So while the Corinthians may have been divided over their allegiance to different leaders (to Peter, Paul, Apollos or Christ himself – see 1 Corinthians 1:10–17), Paul rejects wholeheartedly such divisive attitudes or human rivalry. Apollos is simply another brother in Christ, and Paul urges him to continue his work in Corinth.

Who are the people who have influenced you in your journey of life and faith, working with you, praying for you, encouraging you in the hardest times? Name them now and give thanks for them. The Christian way is not to be pursued alone – we need brothers and sisters in Christ. We need people to alert us to the challenges, to lift us up and help us to 'be courageous' and 'be strong' (v. 13), and to know the love of Christ.

Who are the people who need courage, strength and love today?
Pray for them.

TERRY HINKS

People who refresh our spirits

Now, brothers and sisters, you know that members of the household of Stephanas were the first fruits in Achaia, and they have devoted themselves to the service of the saints; I urge you to put yourselves at the service of such people and of everyone who works and toils with them. I rejoice at the coming of Stephanas and Fortunatus and Achaicus, because they have made up for your absence, for they refreshed my spirit as well as yours. So give recognition to such persons.

Today I want to give thanks for Stephanas and people like him who have played a crucial role in serving God's people down the years. In just a few verses of this great letter we hear about one whom Paul respected and wanted to be recognised and respected by the church he served.

At the beginning of the letter Paul had almost forgotten that he had baptised Stephanas as one of the first converts in the region of Achaia (1 Corinthians 1:16) and rather downplayed his part in that wonderful moment in Stephanas' life. Now he reminds the Corinthians of the importance of Stephanas' coming to faith and how he had served the church faithfully and wholeheartedly ever since. It is probably Stephanas, along with his companions, who brought news and a letter from the Corinthian church to Paul, a letter that then caused Paul to write so vigorously in response. That visit meant much to Paul, a reminder that he was not forgotten and that his advice was much needed by the church. It did indeed 'refresh his spirit'.

Our spirits can so easily get tired, cynical or worn down, burdened by the brokenness of the world around us and within us. We can literally become dis-spirited! How can our spirits be raised and refreshed? And how can we refresh the spirits of other people, sharing the same Christian journey? It is the encouragers, those filled by the Spirit of love and truth, the Spirit of Jesus, who can refresh us. We need to seek them in our faith journey and allow them to refresh our spirits, that we too may be encouragers for others.

Give thanks for Stephanas, alongside the many unnamed and unrecognised saints, who have served God and refreshed spirits.

TERRY HINKS

A final word

The churches of Asia send greetings. Aquila and Prisca, together with the church in their house, greet you warmly in the Lord. All the brothers and sisters send greetings. Greet one another with a holy kiss. I, Paul, write this greeting with my own hand. Let anyone be accursed who has no love for the Lord. Our Lord, come! The grace of the Lord Jesus be with you. My love be with all of you in Christ Jesus.

We arrive at the end of this great letter, which has dealt with many key elements of Christian faith and discipleship. All that has to be done now is to give the final greetings. Paul begins with the church in Ephesus and other Asian churches founded during his ministry there. Then he mentions his dear friends, the couple Aquila and Prisca (or Priscilla) who have worked so hard alongside him. They host a house church whose members also add their salutations. Then Paul looks around at his coworkers and sends their greetings too. Such greetings may have been customary to all such letters of this time, but here they go far beyond mere routine; they are heartfelt and 'in the Lord' (v. 19).

The warmth of this outpouring of love is palpable and so Paul suggests the Corinthian Christians greet each other with the customary 'holy kiss'. Finally, he takes up the pen from the scribe to authenticate the letter in his own hand and with his own personal greeting. These are not just words – they are a blessing and not to be given glibly, far less carelessly. Without love we are nothing, as he said earlier in the letter. The gift becomes a curse if there is no love – either for the Lord or each other. The Lord of love remains the heart of the matter, hence Paul's prayer and the prayer of the early church: 'Our Lord, come!' (v. 22) – in Aramaic, *Maranatha*.

Love is the final word – the grace of our Lord Jesus and the love Paul has for his difficult church in Corinth – not just any love, but a love for all and a love that we see in Jesus.

Imagine Paul sending you his greeting, his love. Then know the grace and love of the Lord Jesus with you today.

TERRY HINKS

If you've enjoyed this set of reflections by **Terry Hinks**,
check out his book published with BRF, including…

Praying the Way
*with Matthew, Mark,
Luke and John*

978 0 85746 716 4
£10.99

To order, visit **brfonline.org.uk** or use the order form at the end.

Gordon on the Jordan

 Rivers are vital to our existence, and many of our greatest cities and oldest lands are defined by their rivers. London has the Thames, Rome the Tiber and Paris the Seine, while Iraq, Syria and Turkey have the Tigris and Euphrates, and Egypt, the Nile. The holy lands of Old and New Testament times have the Jordan, which is still as important as it ever was to modern Israel, Palestine, Syria and Jordan.

Rivers provide life-giving water, naturally, but they are also the highways of the past, on which trade routes and transport depended and operated. They carve their passage, forming ravines and tributaries, and their pathways cut into the landscape in ways that is both geographical and historical: they are four dimensional, having width, depth, volume and history. They move through time and space, flowing like liquid music across the ear and before the eye, and remind us of the old adage that one never steps into the same river twice.

Although it is true that rivers dry up, burst their banks and change their course, bringing both life and death, we also have a paradoxical sense that they are changeless – they have been there a long time, meandering, rising and falling, watering the land for ages. They accommodate plants and fish and other lifeforms we can barely see, a source of food for those who live in or near them. This is true of any river, so it is no surprise that civilisations originated near rivers and great cities remain around them.

Yet the Jordan is not just any river. It is *the* biblical river, which flows through the story of salvation, in which prophets and kings bathed, across which safety was reached and in which Christian baptism was invented. This week let us take a trip down the River Jordan, riding on and across it, to see some familiar sights from a different angle: from the waterline. Let us see if the water conceals murky depths, reflects the light above, or both. For we are in good company: Abraham, Lot, Moses, Joshua, Elijah, Elisha, King David, John and Jesus. All the best people have been to the Jordan. Let us join them, as we time travel up and down river.

GORDON GILES

A damaged Lot

Lot looked about him and saw that the plain of the Jordan was well watered everywhere like the garden of the Lord, like the land of Egypt, in the direction of Zoar; this was before the Lord had destroyed Sodom and Gomorrah. So Lot chose for himself all the plain of the Jordan, and Lot journeyed eastward, and they separated from each other. Abram settled in the land of Canaan, while Lot settled among the cities of the plain and moved his tent as far as Sodom.

This is the first reference in the Bible to the River Jordan, the river that runs through the story of salvation like a silver thread, gleaming with promise, flowing with hope and sometimes concealing murky depths. This passage is about how Lot and Abram go their separate ways, which was necessary to do because, having journeyed together, their flocks and herds have become too numerous for further cohabitation. While in Canaan, Abram generously offers Lot first choice, and he chooses to travel east and settle on the fertile plain of the Jordan. Yet all is not so sunny on this side of the river, and the reference to Sodom and Gomorrah is ominous with hindsight. Lot is infected with the corruption of those places, and even though he eventually leaves, his wife is turned into a pillar of salt because she looks back (Genesis 19:26).

It is not an auspicious start for the River Jordan, whose streams flow past a sordid story. Yet just as the sun shines on the righteous and the wicked, rivers bring their benefits and their catastrophes without fear or favour. In Luke's gospel, Jesus says that, 'Likewise, just as it was in the days of Lot, they were eating and drinking, buying and selling, planting and building, but on the day that Lot left Sodom it rained fire and sulphur from heaven and destroyed all of them' (Luke 17:28–29).

Lot is seen as righteous (2 Peter 2:7) and, like the Jordan itself, the ever so human ambiguity of his life flows to us from an almost hidden past. Lot is tainted by his experiences on the Jordan plain. Yet in Christ, the flowing living water can wash us clean.

In what ways have you been damaged by the behaviour of those with whom you keep or have kept company?

GORDON GILES

Struggle in the stream

[Jacob]… crossed the ford of the Jabbok… A man wrestled with him until daybreak. When the man saw that he did not prevail against Jacob, he struck him on the hip socket, and Jacob's hip was put out of joint as he wrestled with him. Then he said, 'Let me go, for the day is breaking.' But Jacob said, 'I will not let you go, unless you bless me'… Then the man said, 'You shall no longer be called Jacob, but Israel, for you have striven with God and with humans, and have prevailed.'

The Jabbok is now called the Zarqa River and as a tributary of the Jordan can still be visited. In November 2012, a parish pilgrimage bus parked in a layby near a concrete bridge and a group of 40 of us descended to a rather disappointing, muddy brown stream and recalled this remarkable story of Jacob's spiritual and physical tussle. I remember it vividly, and I daresay Jacob did too. It changed his name and his life, and the world.

The name 'Israel' has its very roots in this bankside battle. *El* means 'God' and *'sarah* relates to prevailing over; which is to say that Israel means 'God struggles'. That the Jabbok is a murky tributary of the Jordan reminds us of our relationship to God. We all struggle at times – living and breathing faith is not about having an easy ride without conflict, challenge or commitment.

Jacob reached an uneasy, face-to-face peace with God, emergent from a 'score draw', making it both a victory and a defeat. This truce, which enabled a new relationship and a new name, comes when Jacob is most vulnerable. He is there because he is anxious about his reunion with Esau, whom he had tricked many years earlier. Vulnerability causes struggle, and struggling leads to vulnerability. Through these God strengthens and recalls us to the ultimate truth that, fight as we may, at the end comes blessing and a revelation of divine love.

Can you see the love of God as the outcome of struggles in your life?

GORDON GILES

River view

'Go up to the top of Pisgah and look around you to the west, to the north, to the south, and to the east. Look well, for you shall not cross over this Jordan. But charge Joshua and encourage and strengthen him, because it is he who shall cross over at the head of this people and who shall secure their possession of the land that you will see.'

Here Moses meets God and is shown the land first 'promised' to Abraham, Isaac and Jacob. Yet it is Joshua who will secure it. Pisgah is now identified with Ras as-Siyagha, south-east of Jordan's capital Amman. It is commonly considered to be Mount Nebo, and is associated with Moses' place of death and burial. There is a fantastic view looking across a desert landscape that cannot have changed much since Moses' day.

On top of the mountain is a sculpture depicting a bronze serpent and the cross intertwined. It reminds us of the connection between Moses and Jesus: 'Just as Moses lifted up the serpent in the wilderness, so must the Son of Man be lifted up' (John 3:14). I met someone up there who said his father used to walk to Jerusalem, 28 miles away! Jericho is also visible, 16 miles north-west, as is the Dead Sea, into which the River Jordan flows down from the Sea of Galilee ('Jordan' means 'flow down'). The river ends at the Dead Sea, 422 metres below sea level. Two tributaries enter nearby: the Yarmouk and the Zarqa (Jabbok).

These wind through the wilderness, barely watering the wadis they cross. Yet they have been sufficient to sustain life and civilisation for millennia. In northern Europe we think of long and wide continental rivers, whereas the Jordan is little more than a stream connecting two lakes and now dividing Israel and Jordan, with three main border crossings (the most famous is the King Hussein, or Allenby, Bridge near Jericho).

The Jordan has carved the land of biblical history and its modern life, spiritual, religious and political. It has borne a flow of divine providence, commandment and promise in its path. Ever changing yet changeless, this paradoxical relationship to the holy land and the wider world remains significant and special.

What signs and symptoms of God's promise flow through your life?

GORDON GILES

Safe crossing

The Jordan overflows all its banks throughout the time of harvest. So when those who bore the ark had come to the Jordan and the feet of the priests bearing the ark were dipped in the edge of the water, the waters flowing from above stood still, rising up in a single heap far off at Adam, the city that is beside Zarethan, while those flowing towards the sea of the Arabah, the Dead Sea, were wholly cut off. Then the people crossed over opposite Jericho. While all Israel were crossing over on dry ground, the priests who bore the ark of the covenant of the Lord stood firmly on dry ground in the middle of the Jordan, until the entire nation finished crossing over the Jordan.

Adam was 18 miles north of Jericho, on Jordan's east side, just south of the Jabbok river (see Monday). Any further south becomes harder to cross. The Arabah Sea is the Dead Sea. This all happened at a time of flood, which we might instinctively think is not the best time to cross. *Normally* it was a hundred feet wide and three to ten feet deep, flowing fast and surrounded by thickets in which wild animals sheltered. Crossing it was not exactly safe at the best of times.

We are reminded of Noah's flood (see Genesis 7) and of Moses crossing the Sea of Reeds on dry land (see Exodus 14:21). This crossing begins as the priests arrive. Two other groups – twelve men and the rest of the people – then cross and are saved, literally and metaphorically. Arriving into the promised land on Jordan's opposite bank, they are spared calamity in a journey through swollen floodwaters that could bear any and every one of them away. We have seen flood waters in Mozambique, Pakistan and Bangladesh in recent years – it must be terrifying to be swept away, out of control, at the mercy of the elemental forces of wind and water.

In this story, therefore, God does not make it easy, for the harder the crossing, the greater the need of faith and the deed of power to enable it.

Dare you pray for God's help in the really hard things, or do you confine your prayers to still waters and shallow streams in low season?

GORDON GILES

A momentous mantle

They both were standing by the Jordan. Then Elijah took his mantle and rolled it up and struck the water; the water was parted to the one side and to the other, until the two of them crossed on dry ground… As they continued walking and talking, a chariot of fire and horses of fire separated the two of them, and Elijah ascended in a whirlwind into heaven… He picked up the mantle of Elijah that had fallen from him and went back and stood on the bank of the Jordan. He… struck the water. He said, 'Where is the Lord, the God of Elijah?'… He struck the water again, and the water was parted to the one side and to the other, and Elisha crossed over.

I did a placement in a very rough area and, having arrived quite late, the vicar immediately took me on a night tour of some very deprived council estates and made a point of getting folk to say hello. I was nervous that we were out so late in a high crime area, but he said, 'We need to do this so they recognise you and know that you are with me. Then you will be safe.'

The 'passing of the mantle' from Elijah to Elisha comes as a culmination of a kind of farewell tour for Elijah, in which he introduces his successor around the region (he has already 'appointed' Elisha in 1 Kings 19:19). As part of this journey, Elijah uses his cloak to part the waters, like Moses crossing the sea and Joshua crossing the Jordan. It is important for onlookers that, as Elijah disappears, Elisha identically parts the waters with the same mantle.

It is like a graduation and inauguration rolled into one. For just as everyone knows who the president is to be before they take office formally, and a student knows their exam results before graduating, the ceremonial is important and necessary to formally recognise and mark the moment of transition. Similarly we 'mark' birthdays, festivals, New Year's Day: observing 'magic' moments in which nothing actually happens, but which are nonetheless momentous. Yet for Elisha it is also proof that he is not only the natural successor chosen by Elijah himself, but that God approves.

Who are you with? Whose mantle do you wear?

GORDON GILES

The best river

Naaman came with his horses and chariots and halted at the entrance of Elisha's house. Elisha sent a messenger to him, saying, 'Go, wash in the Jordan seven times, and your flesh shall be restored, and you shall be clean.' But Naaman became angry and went away, saying, 'I thought that for me he would surely come out and stand and call on the name of the Lord his God and would wave his hand over the spot and cure the skin disease! Are not Abana and Pharpar, the rivers of Damascus, better than all the waters of Israel? Could I not wash in them and be clean?' He turned and went away in a rage.

Which river is better: the Thames, the Rhine or the Seine? The Jordan, the Pharpar or the Abana? It is an odd and difficult question and the likelihood is that, if forced to, one would vote for the river of one's own land. It is almost like asking what national team you support. So it is a strange question with an obvious answer.

Naaman would say so, anyway: 'If all I have to do is wash in the river why can't I do it in my own river, thank you very much. And my rivers are much better than yours too!' He is somewhat arrogant, expecting Elisha to emerge and greet him with pleasantries and treat his request to be healed with not only due deference but an appropriate flourish, a hand waved in the air by a stick-wielding shaman accompanied no doubt by an incantation of some kind. Naaman's name means 'gracious', but he does not live up to it here, taking umbrage at what he considers to be Elisha's dismissive, perfunctory instruction.

The River Abana is now called Barada and is the main river of modern Damascus. The Pharpar is now the Awaj, running from Mount Hermon and flows for 43 miles eastwards to Damascus. Naaman's boast is not unfounded however: he would say that these rivers are better than the trickling Jordan, because the hydraulic engineering that had been employed to make them irrigate the land was one of the most sophisticated and extensive in the ancient world.

Do you ever claim spiritual superiority or claim that your faith is better than someone else's?

GORDON GILES

A serious river-washing

But his servants approached and said to him, 'Father, if the prophet had commanded you to do something difficult, would you not have done it? How much more, when all he said to you was, "Wash, and be clean"?' So he went down and immersed himself seven times in the Jordan, according to the word of the man of God; his flesh was restored like the flesh of a young boy, and he was clean. Then he returned to the man of God, he and all his company; he came and stood before him and said, 'Now I know that there is no God in all the earth except in Israel.'

The story of the healing of Naaman is one of the longest stories in the Bible: so we spend two days on it! Throughout history people have expected signs and wonders to accompany miraculous acts, and to some extent feel shortchanged if they do not get them. Jesus had the same problem, and here Elisha is a precursor of the Christ who said, 'Unless you see signs and wonders you will not believe' (John 4:48).

Yet Naaman rather perfunctorily and begrudgingly does what he has been told to do. Elisha is basically saying, 'With my God, I don't need to do much and nor do you. With obedience, discipline and faith, great things can happen even to a great person such as you think yourself to be.' Nevertheless there is conventional behaviour here: a ritual cleansing required a sevenfold act, and Naaman's submissive self-immersion results in not only a conversion of his skin to health, but his spiritual conversion too. Physical cleansing represents and reflects spiritual change. We should not see this as a kind of pre-Christian baptism, yet the parallels are apparent.

Centuries later, John made people submerge themselves in the water, and Jesus did so himself. Jesus also healed ten lepers at once and did so without using water at all (see Luke 17:11–19). Elisha, prophet of God, points us forward to Jesus but is to be completely overshadowed by him, who will be greater than any of the prophets in the tradition of which so many of his significant actions stand.

Does your faith need physical proof or extravagant signs and gestures?

GORDON GILES

Disaster averted

Now the company of prophets said to Elisha... 'Let us go to the Jordan, and let us collect logs there, one for each of us, and build a place there for us to live.' He answered, 'Do so.' Then one of them said, 'Please come with your servants.' And he answered, 'I will.' So he went with them. When they came to the Jordan, they cut down trees. But as one was felling a log, his axehead fell into the water; he cried out, 'Alas, master! It was borrowed.' Then the man of God said, 'Where did it fall?' When he showed him the place, he cut off a stick and threw it in there and made the iron float. He said, 'Pick it up.' So he reached out his hand and took it.

This iron-raising happened when Elisha and his entourage of followers realised that they did not have enough living space and so went to the Jordan to build themselves a new house. No flatpacks for them, but rather basic tools, to cut down trees and hew beams. Doing so, the axe comes apart and the sharp end flies into the water. It is double trouble: the work cannot continue and the axeman has the embarrassing difficulty that the iron age axe was not his to lose.

Elisha to the rescue! We do not know how throwing a piece of wood into water would cause heavy metal to float, so this is a sort of magic. Elisha does not *need* to throw the stick in the water, any more than he needed to throw flour into a pot of poisoned stew in 2 Kings 4:38–41. Yet this is his mode of operation: a miracle involving an action that emphasises the activity of God in physical as well as spiritual terms.

We are more accustomed to believing in God's action in our lives without a magic stick, whereas in Elisha's time it was sometimes expected. The stick points to God and his provision and care, essential to a people wandering in search of safety, shelter and hope. Nowadays we appeal directly to Christ, who was raised on a more significant plank of wood, held in the place of universal redemption by iron nails, to be raised on the third day.

Do you need magic to believe in God?
Reflect on the subtle miracles in your life.

GORDON GILES

The bigger picture

When Israel went out from Egypt, the house of Jacob from a people of strange language, Judah became God's sanctuary, Israel his dominion. The sea looked and fled; Jordan turned back. The mountains skipped like rams, the hills like lambs. Why is it, O sea, that you flee? O Jordan, that you turn back? O mountains, that you skip like rams? O hills, like lambs? Tremble, O earth, at the presence of the Lord, at the presence of the God of Jacob, who turns the rock into a pool of water, the flint into a spring of water.

This wonderful hymn from the Psalter connects the crossings of the Sea of Reeds in Exodus to that of the Jordan in Joshua. Both are miracles of divine intervention over the flowing forces of nature that sea and river present. The psalmist tells of the long march of God's people from Egypt to the promised land and reminds us that both crossings were part of a great overarching plan.

On 26 February, Sally Welch reminded us of Archbishop Desmond Tutu's wonderful saying that the only way to eat an elephant is 'one bite at a time'. Sometimes we see the Old Testament a bit like that – bits and pieces of a story – and forget that it is all part of a bigger journey, a bigger plan. If we concentrate too much on the little bites – the steps of the journey – we can forget that at the end of it all we have actually eaten a whole elephant! Every bite matters and adds up.

Out of a series of terrifying ordeals lasting 40 years comes divinely powerful redemption and joy, provision and plenty.

There is another, second 'exodus', which is the journey to freedom that Christ brings through his death and resurrection. Some see Moses as prefiguring Jesus, who leads his people to freedom (but does not complete the task), which comes to fruition in Christ's saving work. No surprise then that that great hymn written three millennia later helps us see the crossing of the Jordan as a metaphorical journey to resurrection life: 'When I tread the verge of Jordan, bid my anxious fears subside. Death of death, and hell's destruction, land me safe on Canaan's side' (William Williams, 1717–91).

Can you see the big picture of your life's journey stretching behind you?

GORDON GILES

Christ within

And the whole Judean region and all the people of Jerusalem were going out to him and were baptised by him in the River Jordan, confessing their sins… In those days Jesus came from Nazareth of Galilee and was baptised by John in the Jordan. And just as he was coming up out of the water, he saw the heavens torn apart and the Spirit descending like a dove on him. And a voice came from the heavens, 'You are my Son, my Beloved; with you I am well pleased.'

The Jordan has ebbed and flowed through biblical time and place, and does not now flow where it did in Jesus' time, nor in the days of the Old Testament when Lot, Jacob, Moses, Joshua, Elijah, Elisha and Naaman walked its banks. Many accept that the site now known as Bethany by the Jordan, accessible from both the Jordanian and Israeli sides, is the 'holy' site to visit, but it is a few hundred metres away from the place where the Jordan is thought to have flowed in Jesus' day, which is now dry. It can still be visited, and it is strange to stand in a small valley and wonder what it looked like 2,000 years ago, as well to reflect on the fact that the place where the initiation of the one who was himself the source of living water is bone dry.

That the Jordan is somewhere else now teaches us what Jesus taught the Samaritan woman at the well (John 4): that God does not operate only on a mountain, in a temple or in a river, but everywhere. Worship in spirit and truth can be anywhere, especially in the site of our baptism, which is in our hearts and souls. Historical sites are powerful reminders and affect us deeply, but the true location of Jesus, of his presence in each of our lives, is within us.

As we have journeyed through biblical time and geographical space these past days, I hope the river cruise has reflected new light on biblical history as the charting of God's loving power and presence flowing, like the Jordan, through the stories on which our civilisation, culture and faith are built.

Creator God, may your love flow through our lives
and may our faith never be washed away. Amen.

GORDON GILES

SHARING OUR VISION – MAKING A GIFT

**I would like to make a donation to support BRF Ministries.
Please use my gift for:**

☐ Where the need is greatest ☐ Anna Chaplaincy ☐ Living Faith

☐ Messy Church ☐ Parenting for Faith

Title	First name/initials	Surname

Address

	Postcode

Email

Telephone

Signature	Date

Our ministry is only possible because of the generous support of individuals, churches, trusts and gifts in wills.

Please treat as Gift Aid donations all qualifying gifts of money made (*tick all that apply*)   *giftaid it*

☐ today, ☐ in the past four years, ☐ and in the future.

I am a UK taxpayer and understand that if I pay less Income Tax and/or Capital Gains Tax in the current tax year than the amount of Gift Aid claimed on all my donations, it is my responsibility to pay any difference.

☐ My donation does not qualify for Gift Aid.

Please notify us if you want to cancel this Gift Aid declaration, change your name or home address, or no longer pay sufficient tax on your income and/or capital gains.

You can also give online at **brf.org.uk/donate**, which reduces our administration costs, making your donation go further.

Please complete other side of form

SHARING OUR VISION – MAKING A GIFT

Please accept my gift of:

☐ £2 ☐ £5 ☐ £10 ☐ £20 Other £ [　　　　　]

by (*delete as appropriate*):

☐ Cheque/Charity Voucher payable to 'BRF'

☐ MasterCard/Visa/Debit card/Charity card

Name on card

Card no. ☐☐☐☐ ☐☐☐☐ ☐☐☐☐ ☐☐☐☐

Expires end [M M] [Y Y] Security code* ☐☐☐ *Last 3 digits on the reverse of the card

Signature

Date

☐ I would like to leave a gift to BRF Ministries in my will. Please send me further information.

☐ I would like to find out about giving a regular gift to BRF Ministries.

For help or advice regarding making a gift, please contact our fundraising team +44 (0)1865 462305

Your privacy

We will use your personal data to process this transaction. From time to time we may send you information about the work of BRF Ministries that we think may be of interest to you. Our privacy policy is available at **brf.org.uk/privacy**. Please contact us if you wish to discuss your mailing preferences.

Registered with

(FR)

FUNDRAISING **REGULATOR**

☜ Please complete other side of form

Please return this form to 'Freepost BRF'
No other address information or stamp is needed

Bible Reading Fellowship is a charity (233280) and company limited by guarantee (301324), registered in England and Wales

Overleaf… Reading *New Daylight* in a group | Author profile | Recommended reading | Order and subscription forms

Reading New Daylight in a group

GORDON GILES

General discussion starters

These can be used for any study series within this issue. Remember there are no right or wrong answers – these questions are simply to enable a group to engage in conversation.

- What do you think is the main idea or theme of the author in this series? Did that come across strongly?
- Have any of the issues discussed touched on personal – or shared – aspects of your life?
- What evidence or stories do the authors draw on to illuminate, or be illuminated by, the passages of scripture.
- Which do you prefer: scripture informing daily modern life, or modern life shining a new light on scripture?
- Does the author 'call you to action' in a realistic and achievable way? Do you think their ideas will work in the secular world?
- Have any specific passages struck you personally? If so, how and why? Is God speaking to you through scripture and reflection?
- Was anything completely new to you? Any 'eureka' or jaw-dropping moments? If so, what difference will that make?

Questions for specific series

Stephen: Acts 6—7 (Elizabeth Rundle)

- What problems and resistance do today's congregations face?
- What do we need to change as we seek outreach and growth?
- What benefits do deacons and lay workers bring to a church?
- What changes within church life have you found most helpful?
- What are Stephen's main qualities and what positive message does his story convey to us today?

John 5—7 (Liz Hoare)

- Why do you think Jesus remains such a divisive figure even today?
- What fresh insight have you gained into Jesus' relationship with his heavenly Father through the readings?
- What have you discovered about the connection between Jesus and the Hebrew scriptures through studying these passages?
- Where do the images of hunger and thirst resonate most in the world at present?
- What does it mean to hear Jesus say 'whoever comes to me will never be hungry and whoever believes in me shall never be thirsty'?

Parables of passion (Roland Riem)

- What is there to be gained by highlighting the parables in word and deed in Matthew 20—27?
- Which parable or action covered in these readings do you most relate to, and why?
- When you have faced your own suffering, what story has your life told? (Take an example you can share, and don't be hard on yourself – you are not Jesus!)
- Does Passiontide feel any different this year? If so, how and why?

Alive in Christ: 1 Corinthians 15—16 (Terry Hinks)

- Paul hands on the key elements of the Christian faith that have been passed on to him. What are the key elements you would hand on to others? How would you tell the story of the risen Jesus today?
- How was Paul's encounter with the risen Christ different to that of Peter and the first disciples? How do we meet and respond to the risen Jesus today?
- Paul quotes two sayings in 1 Corinthians 15:32–34 (one biblical and one secular). What sayings have influenced you? Are they true?
- Is death an enemy or a friend? What does a 'good death' look like? What does the victory of Jesus over death mean for you?
- The collection for those in need in Jerusalem was important to Paul, both practically and symbolically (1 Corinthians 16:1–4). What is the loving action your Christian community is called to undertake today?

Meet the author: Emma Pennington

Tell us how you became a Christian.

I'm not sure there was a time when I became a Christian, as such. I was brought up in a loving environment and from early on we would go to church. I remember a time, though, when God became more real to me, and I wanted to go to the Sunday services for this reason. We attended our local parish church, which was of a high church tradition with incense and servers, and it was this liturgical aspect of going to church that I loved. I must have been quite young at the time. Confirmation was a very important event in my life and from then on I became more serious about my faith, reading the Bible, saying the rosary and attending church as often as I could. I came to have an increasingly significant role at the services and by the time I was a teenager was MC to most events.

Increasingly I was attracted to cathedrals, where I found the anonymity helpful for a shy teenager and the sublime and spiritual music and architecture echo my sensitive and passionate soul. Each summer I would work at the Associated Examining Board marking examination scripts. It was just at the base of the hill leading up to the serene and awesome cathedral of Guildford. Here I spent my lunch breaks, reading and praying. Again it was a cathedral that drew me to Exeter, where I read English and medieval studies. It was here in its ancient beauty and Benedictine foundation that I found a spiritual home and a place of growth and nourishment.

Who or what have been significant influences on your Christian journey?

It was at university that I was most shaped in my Christian life. I was reading for a BA and part of my English course took me into the realm of medieval writing. It was through these texts that I had a profound experience of God. It felt like falling in love as each of the devotional works I was reading appeared to be written to me and for me. I immersed myself in this contemplative way of being and increasingly sought times of silence, study and pray. One day, after the 8.00 am Eucharist at the cathedral which I had been attending daily, I asked the dean of Exeter, Richard Eyre, whether I could go and speak to him. He had wondered how long it would take till I knocked on his door. From then on he became my spiritual director for over 20 years.

It was Richard who suggested I go on retreat. I'd never heard of such things before, but finding a copy of the Retreat Association magazine, I flicked through the pages until my eye was drawn to the Benedictine community at Burford Priory in Oxfordshire. I fell in love with the place and the people. It was as if I had found my way home. Over the next few years, I would return to the community as often as I could, until in 1994 I at last summoned up the courage to ask if I could join and was welcomed with open arms. Work was underway to adapt the old house into accommodation for both men and women, so I was asked to delay my entrance. I agreed to wait and finish my studies and then see what would work best for them.

My money was starting to run out, so I needed to look for a job to tide me over. Where Canterbury Cathedral did not offer me an interview for the role of verger, St Paul's in London did, and I suddenly found myself heading for the big smoke. Within two weeks of my arrival, a young bass vicar choral started turning up to services where he wasn't singing, and rumours were rife around the cathedral community. The rest is history, and we got married in Exeter Cathedral in 1997.

So what of Burford? Part of me still mourns the loss of that community and way of life and I guess will always do. From the moment I took Jonathan to Burford, they blessed our joy and Abbot Stuart Burns (at the time) presided over our wedding service. But I had to rethink. Quickly I went through the discernment process to become a priest, perhaps too quickly as it has taken me a long time to discover, let alone accept, that I might have a ministry as a priest which could be of service to God and the world. The experience of the love of God and my absolute response which I had known through those medieval texts has never left me, and it is to them that I continue to return through my writing, speaking and preaching today.

Tell us about the current context of your ministry in the church.

After many years of association with and deep love of cathedrals, I now find myself ministering in one of them, Canterbury Cathedral. Both Jonathan and I loved working at St Paul's, and it was always a hope, a dream, to return to that way of life and community. I was installed as canon missioner in March 2019. A year later the cathedral life I had joined was much changed as it had been shaken by Covid, restructuring, financial concerns and staff changeover. But what still grounds me and this remarkable community is the daily, faithful *opus dei* or work of God, the offices which stretch back in a continual line to its Benedictine past. I had always wanted to live a life of service as a Benedictine contemplative; I just could never have imagined how that would have been shaped and fulfilled by God in the end.

Recommended reading

It's never been more important to understand how much God loves us and how much he wants us to love each other.

Loving My Neighbour takes us on a journey through the challenging terrain of how we can truly love one another, individually and in our communities.

Daily Bible readings and reflections from Ash Wednesday to Easter Day explore how we can love in truth, love the vulnerable and the suffering, embrace difference, care for our world, and love ourselves as God loves us. Holy Week brings us back to reflect on Christ on the cross, who loved us to the very end.

The following is an edited extract taken from the reflection for Ash Wednesday, entitled 'The simulacrum of love', written by Sanjee Perera.

> *Then the Lord God formed a man from the dust of the ground and breathed into his nostrils the breath of life, and the man became a living being. Now the Lord God had planted a garden in the east, in Eden; and there he put the man he had formed.*
>
> 1 CORINTHIANS 13:13 (NIV)

Today, many of us may attend an Ash Wednesday service where we are marked by a sooty, dust and cinder cross, meant to represent the burnt ashes of our mortality. It is a mark of penance applied by a priest, often with a reminder: 'Remember that you are dust and to dust you shall return.' This sets the tone for Lent as we reflect on what it means to be pilgrims on the narrow way, followers of Christ.

So, Ash Wednesday seems a perfect time to go back to Genesis, to our creation story that roots us in our common humanity, made of star dust and divine breath – dust that made the mostly carbon lifeforms we are. This was kindled into life by a word so potent and creative that the divine breath that awoke us still reverberates through us, and calls to us.

But is this shared humanity and cosmic genesis our core truth? And what does it mean for the way we live in this fallen world on our dying planet, that we were made in the image of love and made stewards of a garden? In Genesis 3:9, when God seeks out his creation, this image bearer of the divine, he calls out, 'Where are you?' Adam replies, 'I heard you in the garden, and I was afraid because I was naked; so I hid' (v. 10). Even then in the grace of Eden, humankind fails to see our kinship to this fount of perfect love, or reveal our naked selves, corrupt and culpable, in the gaze of that perfect glory. And this divine question has echoed through the ages: 'Where are you? What have you done?' Like Adam, our reaction to the challenge of living and loving in truth is often fear and self-preservation.

Recently a headline in *The Sunday Times* read: 'Our interest counts more than migrant needs.' It argued that this was about competing human rights, those of citizens and those outside the polis. In Genesis 4:9, the Lord asks Cain, 'Where is your brother?' and Cain asks the Lord, 'Am I my brother's keeper?' Our incapacity to love in truth has haunted us from our genesis. And the Lord reprimands us as he reprimands Cain, 'What have you done? Listen! Your brother's blood cries out to me from the ground' (v. 10). From the beginning God has made clear the truth of love and justice is that our lives are bound in a selfless love in servanthood and sacrifice to one another.

We live in a world where many don't believe in a shared humanity, let alone a divine genesis, and submitting to the reflective discipline found in the wilderness of Lent seems an unnecessary exercise. We live in an age where we no longer need to depend on each other, where there is an app for everything and artificial intelligence can manage our needs and comfort. We have Google and Siri to answer life's big questions and Alexa to locate that cup of sugar we need. Neighbours are an awkward inconvenience in grating proximity.

And yet we live in a world where infants are washed ashore on our beaches, and refugees fleeing the shark teeth of danger drown in the English Channel. We have learnt to blind ourselves to this world where children go hungry and the vulnerable and elderly die of cold. We live among those forced into modern slavery, and yet look away. This is alien to the core truth of our humanity that was made to mirror that perfect love, a simulacrum of the divine.

Then the salt in the ashen cross reminds us of Jesus' words: we are the salt of the earth. We are called to season the tasteless morsels of life and enrich the banquet. We are the city on the hill, the light of the world and called to love above all else. This is our simulacrum, our truth, our purpose and our salvation.

To order a copy of this book, please use the order form or visit **brfonline.org.uk**

When we feel lost and unmoored, we can turn to God, who reveals himself through powerful metaphors that convey who he is and how he's made us. These images pulse with life, beauty and truth. We explore all creation praising God – the flowers of the field, streams in the desert and trees clapping their hands. Agricultural patterns of sowing, growing and harvesting produce a bounty of meaning for us to receive. Other images include those of God as our help and refuge – our shade and rear guard – and of the change that happens as he clothes us, renews our minds and strengthens us. As we immerse ourselves in these reflections and illustrations, we come to know God more intimately and find hope in him.

Holding Onto Hope
40 days of God's encouragement through art and reflections
Amy Boucher Pye and Leo Boucher
978 1 80039 200 7 £12.99
brfonline.org.uk

To order

Online: brfonline.org.uk
Telephone: +44 (0)1865 319700
Mon–Fri 9.30–17.00

Delivery times within the UK are normally 15 working days. Prices are correct at the time of going to press but may change without prior notice.

Title	Price	Qty	Total
Holding Onto Hope	£12.99		
Loving My Neighbour (BRF Lent book)	£9.99		
Mentoring Conversations	£9.99		
Working from a Place of Rest (new edition)	£9.99		
Praying the Way	£10.99		

POSTAGE AND PACKING CHARGES			
Order value	UK	Europe	Rest of world
Under £7.00	£2.00	Available on request	Available on request
£7.00–29.99	£3.00		
£30.00 and over	FREE		

Total value of books	
Postage and packing	
Donation*	
Total for this order	

* Please complete and return the Gift Aid declaration on page 141.

Please complete in BLOCK CAPITALS

Title _____ First name/initials _____ Surname _____

Address _____

_____ Postcode _____

Acc. No. _____ Telephone _____

Email _____

Method of payment

❑ Cheque (made payable to BRF) ❑ MasterCard / Visa

Card no. ⬚⬚⬚⬚ ⬚⬚⬚⬚ ⬚⬚⬚⬚ ⬚⬚⬚⬚

Expires end ⬚⬚ ⬚⬚ Security code ⬚⬚⬚ Last 3 digits on the reverse of the card

We will use your personal data to process this order. From time to time we may send you information about the work of BRF. Please contact us if you wish to discuss your mailing preferences **brf.org.uk/privacy**

Please return this form to:

BRF Ministries, 15 The Chambers, Vineyard, Abingdon OX14 3FE | **enquiries@brf.org.uk**
For terms and cancellation information, please visit **brfonline.org.uk/terms**.

Bible Reading Fellowship (BRF) is a charity (233280) and company limited by guarantee (301324), registered in England and Wales

BRF Ministries needs you!

If you're one of our many thousands of regular *New Daylight* readers, you will know all about the impact that regular Bible reading has on your faith and the value of daily notes to guide, inform and inspire you.

Here are some recent comments from *New Daylight* readers:

'Thank you for all the many inspiring writings that help so much when things are tough.'

'Just right for me – I learned a lot!'

'We looked forward to each day's message as we pondered each passage and comment.'

If you have similarly positive things to say about *New Daylight*, would you be willing to share your experience with others? Perhaps you could give a short talk or write a brief article about why you find *New Daylight* so helpful. You could form a *New Daylight* reading group, perhaps supplying members with their first copy of the notes. Or you could pass on your back copies or give someone a gift subscription. However you do it, the important thing is to find creative ways to put a copy of *New Daylight* into someone else's hands.

It doesn't need to be complicated and we can help with group and bulk-buy discounts.

We can supply further information if you need it and and would love to hear about it if you do find ways to get *New Daylight* into new readers' hands.

For more information:

- Email **enquiries@brf.org.uk**
- Phone us on **+44 (0)1865 319700** Mon–Fri 9.30–17.00
- Write to us at BRF Ministries, 15 The Chambers, Vineyard, Abingdon OX14 3FE

Inspiring people of all ages to grow in Christian faith

At BRF Ministries, we long for people of all ages to grow in faith and understanding of the Bible. That's what all our work as a charity is about.

- Our **Living Faith** range of resources helps Christians go deeper in their understanding of scripture, in prayer and in their walk with God. Our conferences and events bring people together to share this journey, while our Holy Habits resources help whole congregations grow together as disciples of Jesus, living out and sharing their faith.

- We also want to make it easier for local churches to engage effectively in ministry and mission – by helping them bring new families into a growing relationship with God through **Messy Church** or by supporting churches as they nurture the spiritual life of older people through **Anna Chaplaincy**.

- Our **Parenting for Faith** team coaches parents and others to raise God-connected children and teens, and enables churches to fully support them.

Do you share our vision?

Though a significant proportion of BRF's funding is generated through our charitable activities, we are dependent on the generous support of individuals, churches and charitable trusts.

If you share our vision, would you help us to enable even more people of all ages to grow in faith? Your prayers and financial support are vital for the work that we do. You could:

- support us with a regular donation or one-off gift
- consider leaving a gift to BRF Ministries in your will
- encourage your church to support us as part of your church's giving to home mission – perhaps focusing on a specific ministry or programme
- most important of all, support us with your prayers.

Donate at **brf.org.uk/donate** or use the form on pages 141–42.

A friend indeed

I no longer call you servants, because a servant does not know his master's business. Instead, I have called you friends, for everything that I learned from my Father I have made known to you. You did not choose me, but I chose you and appointed you so that you might go and bear fruit – fruit that will last – and so that whatever you ask in my name the Father will give you.
JOHN 15:15–16 (NIV)

In this verse Jesus is speaking to his disciples in the upper room, a farewell and a sending out, words of comfort and empowerment to get them through the coming days. Here he makes it explicit, those gathered in the room are his friends. Their relationship has transcended that of master and servant through the sharing of knowledge. For a servant simply follows the orders of the master while a friend with profound understanding can take initiative and carry ideas forward – and ultimately bear lasting fruit.

For over 100 years, BRF Ministries has been working to share the knowledge of the gospel with as many people of all ages as possible – from Living Faith resources, such as our *New Daylight* Bible reading notes, to the work of our other ministries: Anna Chaplaincy, Messy Church and Parenting for Faith. It is our goal not only to share the Bible but to give people the tools for deeper understanding and for building a friendship with God that they can then take forward and, in their own lives and communities, bear fruit.

Our work is made possible through kind donations from individuals, charitable trusts and gifts in wills. If you would like to support our work you can become a Friend of BRF by making a monthly gift of £2 a month or more – we thank you for your friendship.

Judith Moore
Fundraising development officer

Give. Pray. Get involved.
brf.org.uk

NEW DAYLIGHT SUBSCRIPTION RATES

Please note our new subscription rates, current until 30 April 2025:

Individual subscriptions
covering 3 issues for under 5 copies, payable in advance
(including postage & packing):

	UK	Europe	Rest of world
New Daylight	£19.50	£26.85	£30.75
New Daylight 3-year subscription (9 issues) (not available for Deluxe)	£57.60	N/A	N/A
New Daylight Deluxe per set of 3 issues p.a.	£24.75	£33.15	£39.15

Group subscriptions
covering 3 issues for 5 copies or more, sent to one UK address (post free):

New Daylight £14.97 per set of 3 issues p.a.

New Daylight Deluxe £19.05 per set of 3 issues p.a.

Please note that the annual billing period for group subscriptions runs from 1 May to 30 April.

Overseas group subscription rates
Available on request. Please email **enquiries@brf.org.uk**.

Copies may also be obtained from Christian bookshops:

New Daylight £4.99 per copy

New Daylight Deluxe £6.35 per copy

All our Bible reading notes can be ordered online
by visiting **brfonline.org.uk/subscriptions**

 New Daylight is also available as an app for Android, iPhone and iPad **brfonline.org.uk/apps**

NEW DAYLIGHT INDIVIDUAL SUBSCRIPTION FORM

All our Bible reading notes can be ordered online by visiting
brfonline.org.uk/subscriptions

Title _____ First name/initials _____ Surname _____

Address _____

_____ Postcode _____

Telephone _____ Email _____

Please send *New Daylight* beginning with the May 2024 / September 2024 / January 2025 issue (*delete as appropriate*):

(*please tick box*)	UK	Europe	Rest of world
New Daylight 1-year subscription	☐ £19.50	☐ £26.85	☐ £30.75
New Daylight 3-year subscription	☐ £57.60	N/A	N/A
New Daylight Deluxe	☐ £24.75	☐ £33.15	☐ £39.15

Optional donation to support the work of BRF Ministries £ _____

Total enclosed £ _____ (cheques should be made payable to 'BRF')

Please complete and return the Gift Aid declaration on page 141 to make your donation even more valuable to us.

Please charge my MasterCard / Visa with £ _____

Card no. ☐☐☐☐ ☐☐☐☐ ☐☐☐☐ ☐☐☐☐

Expires end ☐☐ ☐☐   Security code ☐☐☐   Last 3 digits on the reverse of the card

To set up a Direct Debit, please complete the Direct Debit instruction on page 159.

We will use your personal data to process this order. From time to time we may send you information about the work of BRF Ministries. Please contact us if you wish to discuss your mailing preferences **brf.org.uk/privacy**

Please return this form with the appropriate payment to:
BRF Ministries, 15 The Chambers, Vineyard, Abingdon OX14 3FE
For terms and cancellation information, please visit **brfonline.org.uk/terms**.

Bible Reading Fellowship is a charity (233280) and company limited by guarantee (301324), registered in England and Wales

ND0124

NEW DAYLIGHT GIFT SUBSCRIPTION FORM

☐ I would like to give a gift subscription (please provide both names and addresses):

Title .... First name/initials .... Surname ....

Address ....

.... Postcode ....

Telephone .... Email ....

Gift subscription name ....

Gift subscription address ....

.... Postcode ....

Gift message (20 words max. or include your own gift card):

....

....

Please send *New Daylight* beginning with the May 2024 / September 2024 / January 2025 issue (*delete as appropriate*):

(*please tick box*)	UK	Europe	Rest of world
New Daylight 1-year subscription	☐ £19.50	☐ £26.85	☐ £30.75
New Daylight 3-year subscription	☐ £57.60	N/A	N/A
New Daylight Deluxe	☐ £24.75	☐ £33.15	☐ £39.15

Optional donation to support the work of BRF Ministries £ ....

Total enclosed £ .... (cheques should be made payable to 'BRF')

Please complete and return the Gift Aid declaration on page 141 to make your donation even more valuable to us.

Please charge my MasterCard / Visa with £ ....

Card no. ☐☐☐☐ ☐☐☐☐ ☐☐☐☐ ☐☐☐☐

Expires end ☐☐☐☐ Security code ☐☐☐ Last 3 digits on the reverse of the card

To set up a Direct Debit, please complete the Direct Debit instruction on page 159.

We will use your personal data to process this order. From time to time we may send you information about the work of BRF Ministries. Please contact us if you wish to discuss your mailing preferences **brf.org.uk/privacy**

Please return this form with the appropriate payment to:
BRF Ministries, 15 The Chambers, Vineyard, Abingdon OX14 3FE
For terms and cancellation information, please visit **brfonline.org.uk/terms**.

Bible Reading Fellowship is a charity (233280) and company limited by guarantee (301324), registered in England and Wales

You can pay for your annual subscription to our Bible reading notes using Direct Debit. You need only give your bank details once, and the payment is made automatically every year until you cancel it. If you would like to pay by Direct Debit, please use the form opposite, entering your BRF account number under 'Reference number'.

You are fully covered by the Direct Debit Guarantee:

The Direct Debit Guarantee

- This Guarantee is offered by all banks and building societies that accept instructions to pay Direct Debits.

- If there are any changes to the amount, date or frequency of your Direct Debit, Bible Reading Fellowship will notify you 10 working days in advance of your account being debited or as otherwise agreed. If you request Bible Reading Fellowship to collect a payment, confirmation of the amount and date will be given to you at the time of the request.

- If an error is made in the payment of your Direct Debit, by Bible Reading Fellowship or your bank or building society, you are entitled to a full and immediate refund of the amount paid from your bank or building society.

- If you receive a refund you are not entitled to, you must pay it back when Bible Reading Fellowship asks you to.

- You can cancel a Direct Debit at any time by simply contacting your bank or building society. Written confirmation may be required. Please also notify us.

Instruction to your bank or building society to pay by Direct Debit

Please fill in the whole form using a ballpoint pen and return with order form to:

BRF Ministries, 15 The Chambers, Vineyard, Abingdon OX14 3FE

Service User Number: | 5 | 5 | 8 | 2 | 2 | 9 |

Name and full postal address of your bank or building society

To: The Manager	Bank/Building Society
Address	
	Postcode

Name(s) of account holder(s)

Branch sort code

| | | - | | | - | | |

Bank/Building Society account number

| | | | | | | | |

Reference number

| | | | | | | |

Instruction to your Bank/Building Society

Please pay Bible Reading Fellowship Direct Debits from the account detailed in this instruction, subject to the safeguards assured by the Direct Debit Guarantee. I understand that this instruction may remain with Bible Reading Fellowship and, if so, details will be passed electronically to my bank/building society.

Signature(s)

Banks and Building Societies may not accept Direct Debit instructions for some types of account.

Ministries

Inspiring people of all ages to grow in Christian faith

BRF Ministries is the home of Anna Chaplaincy, Living Faith, Messy Church and Parenting for Faith

As a charity, our work would not be possible without fundraising and gifts in wills.
To find out more and to donate,
visit brf.org.uk/give or call +44 (0)1235 462305